Quilts of the SOUTHWEST

J. Michelle Watts

American Quilter's Society
P.O. Box 3290 • Paducah, KY 42002-3290
www.AmericanQuilter.com

Located in Paducah, Kentucky, the American Quilter's Society (AQS) is dedicated to promoting the accomplishments of today's quilters. Through its publications and events, AQS strives to honor today's quiltmakers and their work and to inspire future creativity and innovation in quiltmaking.

Editor: Toni Toomey
Copy Editor: Chrystal Abhalter
Graphic Design: Amy Chase
Cover Design: Michael Buckingham
Quilt Photos: Charles R. Lynch

Library of Congress Cataloging-in-Publication Data

Watts, J. Michelle, 1959-
Quilts of the Southwest / by J. Michelle Watts.
p. cm.
Summary: "Instructions and step-by-step illustrations for quilt projects influenced by culture, landscape and colors found in the southwest region of the United States of America"--Provided by publisher.
ISBN 1-57432-889-1
1. Patchwork--Southwestern States--Patterns. 2. Quilting--Southwestern States--Patterns. 3. Appliqué--Southwestern States--Patterns. I. Title

TT835.W37598 2005
746.46'041--dc22
2005025640

Additional copies of this book may be ordered from the American Quilter's Society, PO Box 3290, Paducah, KY 42002-3290, or call 1-800-626-5420 or online at www.AmericanQuilter.com.

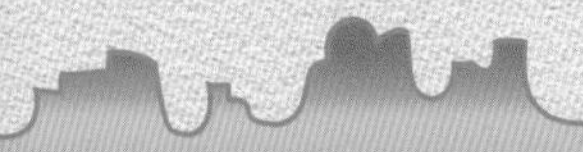

Dedication

I would like to dedicate this book to my husband, Randy, and to my daughter, Jessica. Words cannot express my gratitude for your loving support, patience, and encouragement. Thank you for understanding my passion for quilting. I am blessed to share my life with you. I love you both with all my heart.

Acknowledgments

I would like to thank my grandmother, Cloye Rich, for introducing me to quilting at a very young age. I remember many nights spent with you, sleeping with a quilt frame hanging over us. I believe my interest in quilting was a result of dreaming under your quilts. I am forever grateful.

I would like to thank all my family and friends for all their support, advice, and encouragement.

I would like to thank my friends, Alexis, Glenda, Jan, and Marion for making several of the quilts in this book. You are all so talented, and I am blessed to have friends like you.

I would like to thank Rita Galaska, Phyllis Kent, Richard Larson, and Edith Stanton for doing such incredible machine quilting on many of the quilts. I am grateful to have such creative people to work with.

I would like to thank Casa Talavera, Ltd.; Creations by Sarah; Interiors, Etc.; and the Hurd La Rinconada Gallery and Guest Home for allowing me to take photos on location.

I would like to thank Mary Jo McCarthy for her advice. We both share a love of the Southwest.

Contents

Introduction

As a quilt designer and artist, I am blessed to be surrounded by a wealth of inspiration. My vision as a quilter has been to develop a body of work that would be unique and express my own individual vision. I have been designing and lovingly creating my own style of southwestern quilts for over 15 years. Since the first time I put my pencil to graph paper and designed my first southwestern quilt, I have dreamed of writing this book.

The vast clear blue sky, lonely landscape, and timeless beauty of the southwestern deserts have inspired generations of artists. I am no different. Native American, Spanish, Hispanic, and Anglo artists have created masterpieces that reflect the unique beauty they have experienced. They have given us the opportunity to see this beauty through their eyes. I am so excited to be able to share the beauty I see through the quilts in this book. Southwestern-style quilts are like the Amish quilts of the Northeast and the Hawaiian quilts of the paradise state of Hawaii. Each style incorporates something unique and makes an unforgettable statement. The romance of the southwestern lifestyle has allured people from all over the world. Many visitors come for a week and stay for the rest of their lives. They realize there is something magical, mystical, and simply irresistible about the home of an ancient people. One doesn't have to know a thing about southwestern geography, history, or culture to be intrigued with this style of quilts.

Come join me on a journey through the Southwest and experience what makes this region so unique. I look forward to sharing my passion for southwestern design with you. The quilts featured in my book are inspired by Native American and Spanish weavings, pottery, woven baskets, jewelry, art, beadwork, tinwork, wood carving, and Mexican tile, as well as the stunning elements of southwest landscape and architecture. I hope you enjoy the beautiful photographs scattered throughout the book, because I want to share some of the inspirations for my quilts.

In the first chapter, you will find general construction tips. The projects in this book are created using simple rotary cutting, machine piecing, and fused appliqué techniques. I have included a variety of appliquéd and pieced projects. Whether you are an intermediate or an experienced quilter, the easy to follow, step-by-step instructions guide you to the successful completion of your selected project.

There are eight different pieced projects for you to choose from. LATILLA was inspired by the handcrafted log ceiling found in the home of a friend. RIO GRANDE is a placemat and table runner ensemble that is sure to spice up any table. SQUASH BLOSSOM is a simple pieced block combined with a wide pieced sashing. A secondary design appears when the two are combined. MIDNIGHT IN SANTA FE is a medallion quilt that uses several different design elements found in traditional southwestern weavings and pottery.

There are four wonderful appliqué projects featured in this book. ANCIENT ACOMA is a contemporary wallhanging inspired by a small piece of ancient broken pottery. BEARS AND BEAR PAWS combines the traditional pieced Bear Paw block with an appliquéd bear fetish design. FEATHERED PLATES is a southwestern twist on the traditional Dresden Plate block.

Enjoy your enchanting journey and may the spirit of the Southwest capture your heart.

Tips on Piecing

Begin with a pair of squares.

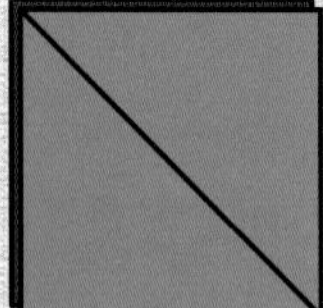

Layer squares right sides together.

Mark a diagonal line through the center of the top square.

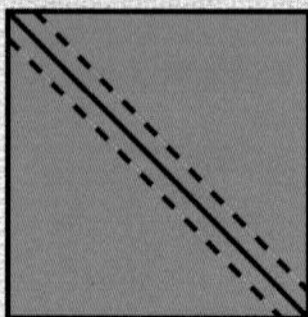

Sew diagonal seam lines ¼" from the center drawn line.

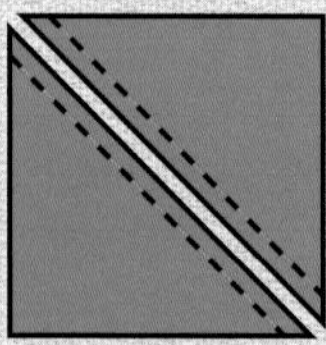

Cut the squares in half along the drawn line.

Each pair of squares yields 2 half-square triangles.

Fig. 1. Piecing half-square triangle units

Throughout this book, I use three traditional piecing techniques—strip-sets, half-square triangles, and corner-squares. These units lend themselves to the geometric patterns in southwestern designs and are easy to piece. The pattern directions were written assuming that you are familiar with basic quilting techniques. Nonetheless, these tips may prove useful to you.

To get your blocks and quilt top to come out the desired size, keep in mind that the more seams you have in a quilt, the more important it is to keep your seam allowances at exactly ¼". To help keep your seam allowances accurate, you can place a piece of moleskin or Post-It® notes as a guide on the machine bed next to or in front of the feed dogs ¼" from the needle.

Half-Square Triangles

To piece half-square triangle units, layer two squares (sizes given in the instructions), right sides together, with the lightest square on top. Draw a diagonal line on the wrong side of the top square. Sew diagonal seams ¼" from both sides of the drawn line. Cut on the drawn line. Each pair of squares yields two half-square triangle units.

Corner-Square Units

Corner-square piecing is the same technique used for sewing a Flying Geese block pieced with two squares and a rectangle (fig. 2). Draw a diagonal line on the wrong side of each square. Place the square on the rectangle with right sides together and sew on the diagonal line. Trim away the excess fabric, leaving a ¼" seam allowance. Press the seam allowances open. Repeat for the other end of the rectangle. Sizes are given in the pattern instructions, but notice that the finished size of your corner-square unit matches the size of the original rectangle.

Variations on the corner-square unit can include sewing squares to one or more corners of any size rectangle or larger square. When sewing four corner squares, add the squares to opposite corners (fig. 3).

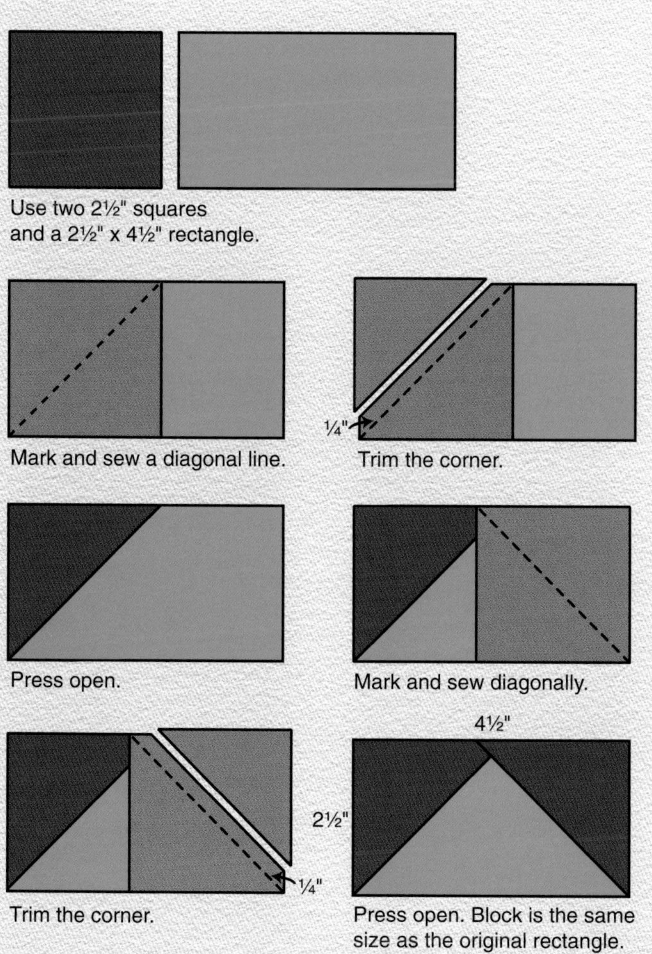

Fig. 2. Piecing a Flying Geese block with the corner-square technique

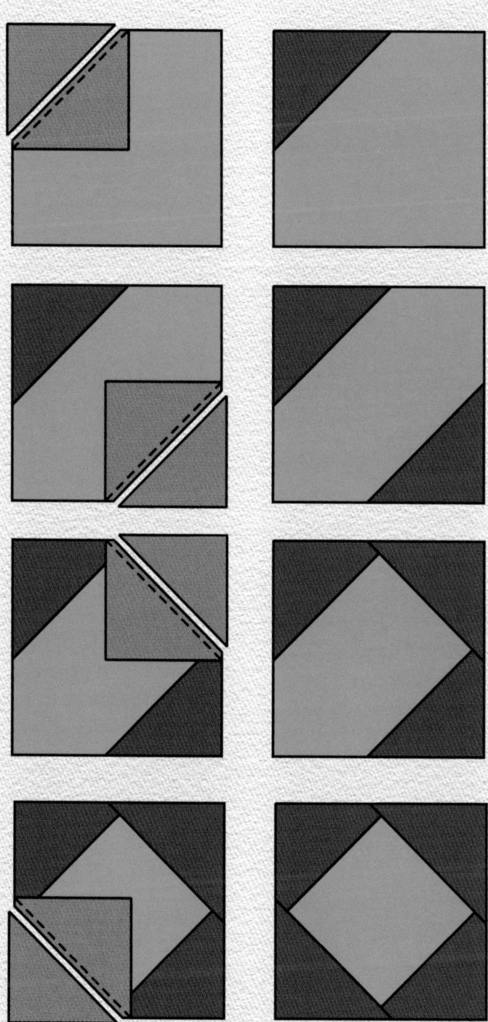

Fig. 3. Sewing a four-corner-square unit

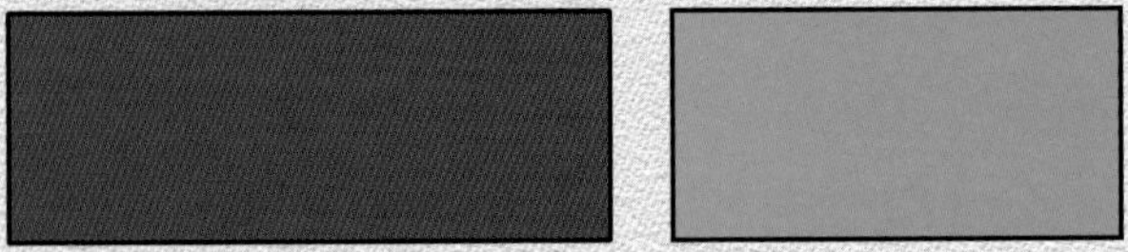

The corner-square technique can be used when the corner piece added is not a square.

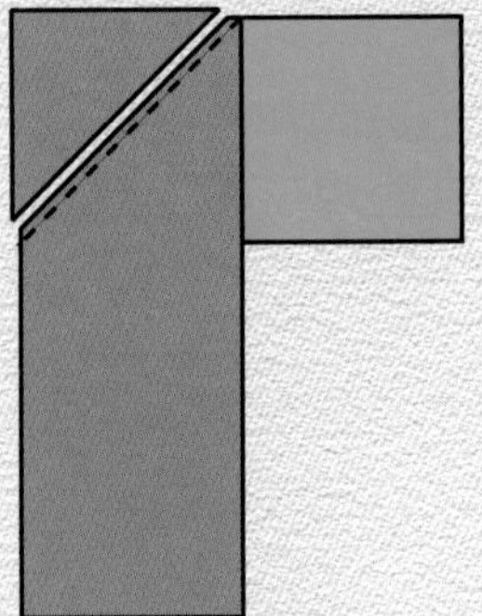

Sew and trim the first rectangle.

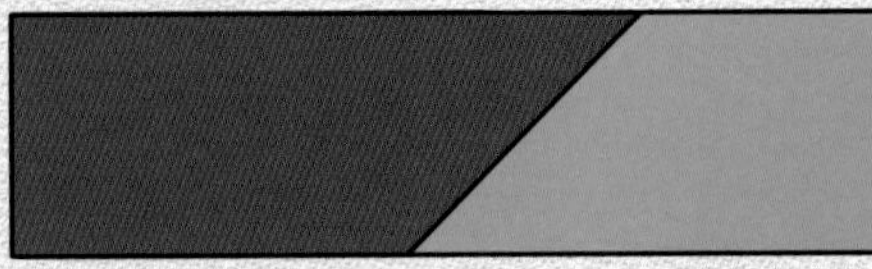

Press open.

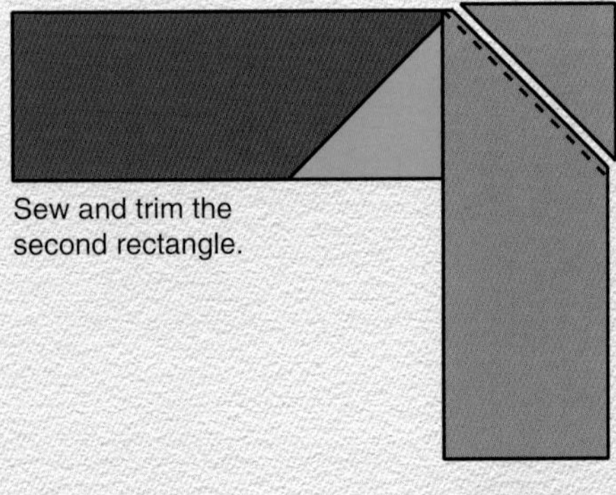

Sew and trim the second rectangle.

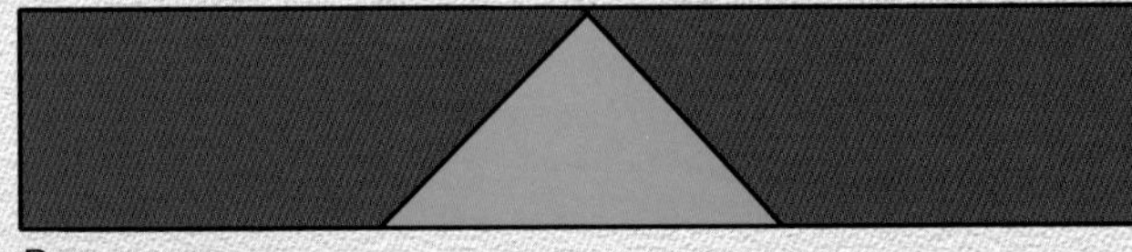

Press open.

Fig. 4. Corner-square technique applied to rectangles

Sometimes the corners are not squares, but the corner-square technique still applies, as shown in figure 4.

Strip Piecing

There are two steps in the strip-piecing technique: Sew thc strips together into strip-sets, then cut the strip-sets into segments (fig. 5).

As shown in figure 6, the widths of the strips and segments are given in the figures that go with the instructions. Unless otherwise noted in the instructions, strip-sets are sewn from 42" strips cut on the width of fabric.

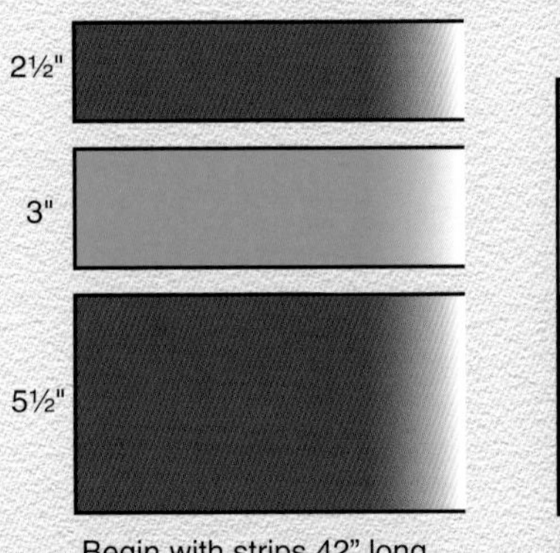

Begin with strips 42" long. Measurements show the cut widths of the strips.

Piece the strips into one long strip-set.

Fig 5. The strip-piecing technique

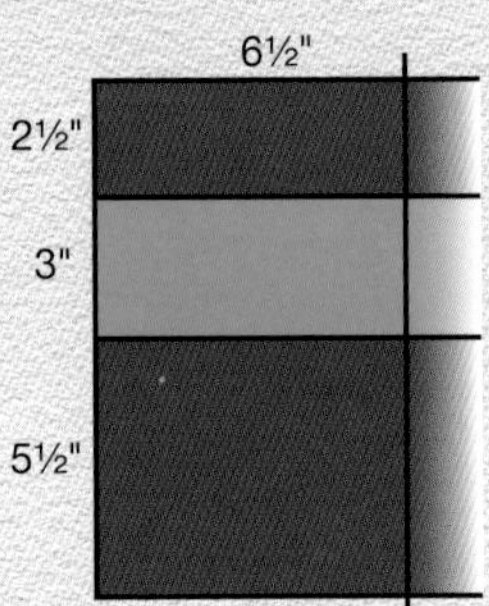

Fig. 6. Condensed instructions show the cut widths of strips and segments.

Crystal

CRYSTAL, 52" x 76". Made by the author. Machine quilted by Rita Galaska, Alto, New Mexico.

This very unique design was inspired by an old Spanish weaving from the late 1800s. When I first saw it, I thought it resembled the traditional Trip Around the World pattern, with a little southwestern flair. The early Spanish settlers to the Rio Grande Valley developed a unique style with countless variations. The serrate concentric diamond designs found in the Saltillo (or Crystal) weavings really caught my eye. It was a challenge to figure out how to make one of these spectacular weavings into a quilt.

Fabric requirements and cutting

Yardages are based on 42" wide fabric. All strips are cut across the width of the fabric.

Olive Green 2 yd

Cut 15 strips 4½" x 42"
From these, cut
4 strips 4½" x 16½"
22 strips 4½" x 12½"
8 strips 4½" x 10½"
4 strips 4½" x 8½"
8 strips 4½" x 6½"
6 strips 4½" x 2½"

Cream Batik Print 2 yd

Cut 14 strips 4½" x 42"
From these, cut
2 strips 4½" x 16 ½"
30 strips 4½" x 12½"
4 strips 4½" x 10½"
2 strips 4½" x 8½"
4 strips 4½" x 6½"
8 strips 4½" x 2½"

Teal Blue 1⅝

Cut 22 strips 2½" x 42"
From these, cut
332 squares 2½" x 2½"

Batting 58" x 82"

Backing 3½ yd
(2 lengths 60", pieced horizontally)

Backing ⅝ yd (7 strips 2½" x 42")

Making Your Crystal Quilt

1. Use 2½" teal squares and the green rectangles shown in figure 1 to piece corner-square units A through F. (See Tips on Piecing Corner-Square Units on page 9.) Press the seam allowances open.

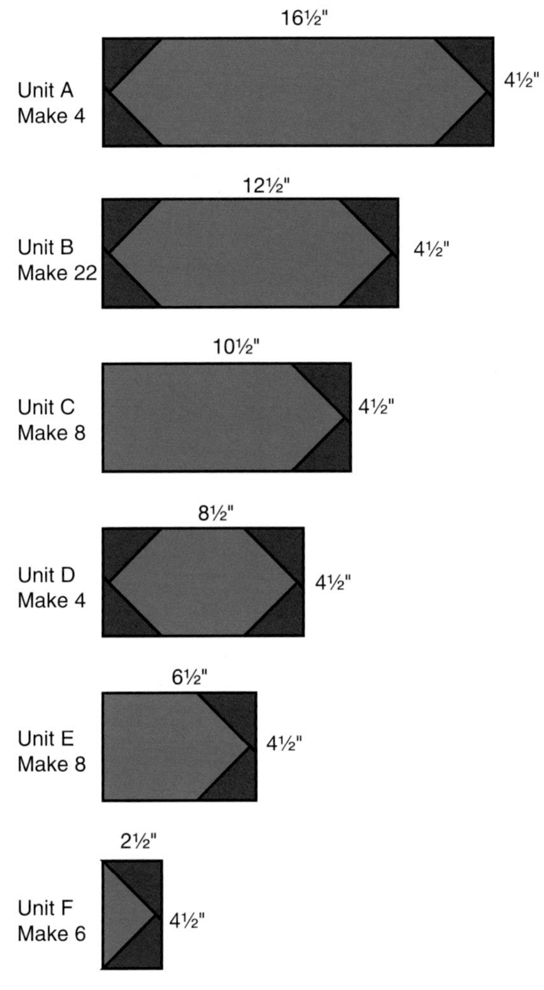

Fig. 1. Piece units A through F.

2. Use the cream strips and 2½" teal squares to piece units G through L (fig. 2). Press the seam allowances open.

3. Assemble rows 1 through 6 as shown in figure 3. Press the seam allowances in one direction.

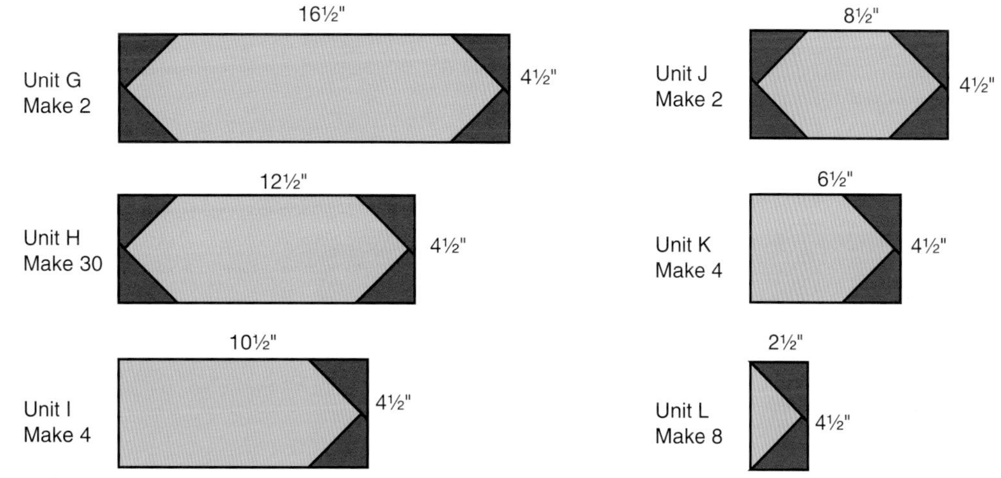

Fig. 2. Piece units G through L.

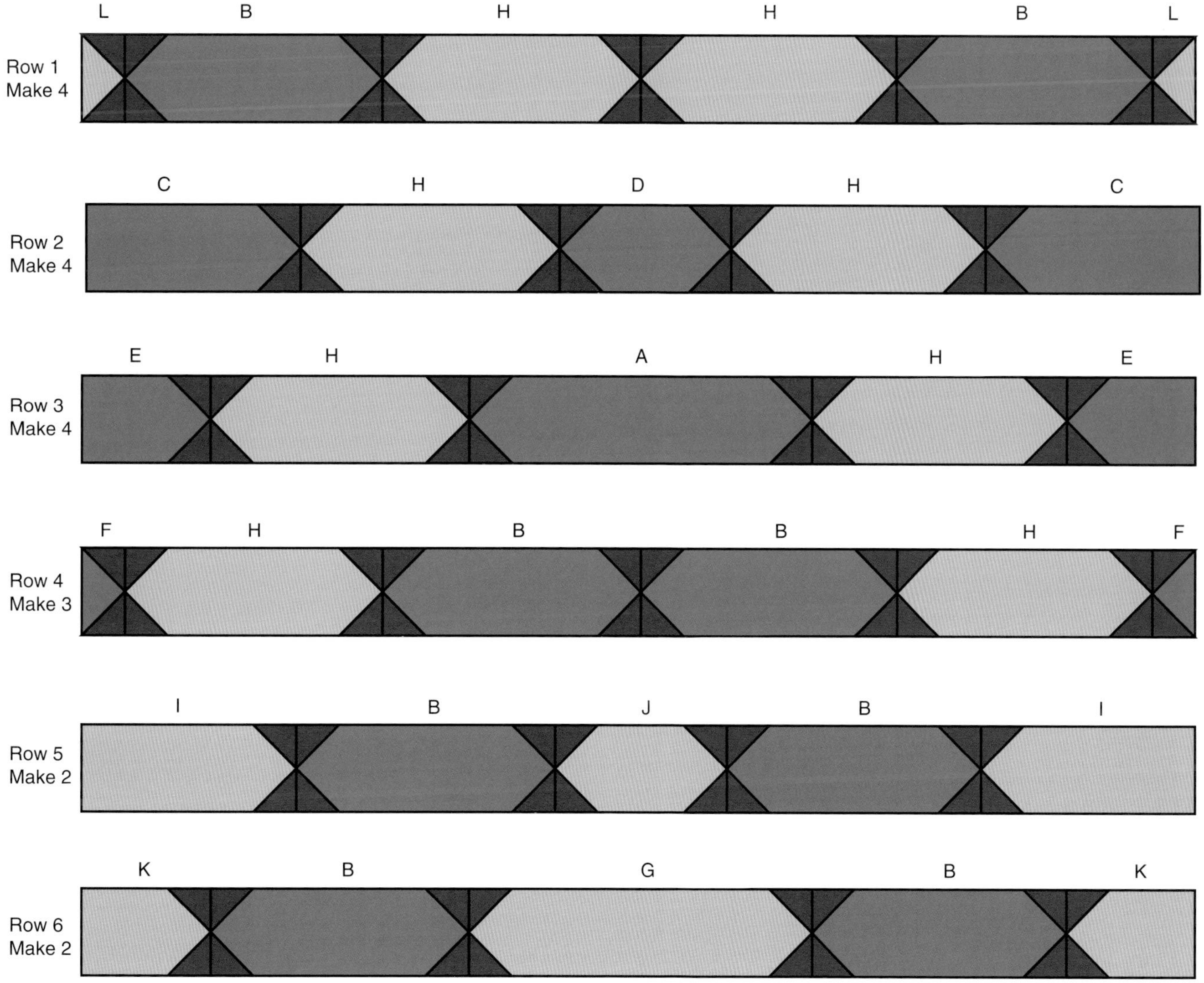

Fig. 3. Assemble rows 1 through 6.

4. Join the rows according to the quilt assembly diagram. Press the seam allowances in one direction.

5. Layer quilt top, batting and backing. Baste layers together. Quilt as desired. Bind edges to finish.

CRYSTAL quilt assembly

BUTTERFLIES AND CRYSTAL, 52" x 76". Made by Alexis Swoboda, Roswell, New Mexico.

Midnight in Santa Fe

A Southwestern Medallion

MIDNIGHT IN SANTA FE — A SOUTHWESTERN MEDALLION, 96" x 100". Pieced by the author and machine quilted by Rita Galaska, Alto, New Mexico.

The geometric designs used by generations of weavers, potters, jewelers, and architects were the inspiration for this stunning medallion-style quilt.

Making Midnight in Santa Fe

The following table gives the total yardage for the complete MIDNIGHT IN SANTA FE quilt.

Total Yardage

Black	9 yd
Wine	¼ yd
Turquoise Green	2⅞ yd
Gold	⅓ yd
Turquoise Blue	½ yd
Olive Green	1 yd
Red	1 yd
Eggplant	1 yd
Melon	⅛ yd
Batting	102" x 106"
Backing (3 lengths 102" long, pieced horizontally)	9 yd
Binding	¾ yd (10 strips 2½" x 42")

Traditional medallion quilts usually start with a center square, and then a variety of borders are added to complete the quilt. The center medallion and the successive borders in MIDNIGHT IN SANTA FE allow you the freedom to make five quilts of different sizes, from a 24½" x 24½" wallhanging to an entire 96" x 100" quilt. To make a quilt the size you want, begin with the medallion in the center and simply stop after the border of your choice. To make the entire quilt with its five borders, follow the cutting instructions in the tables for each section of the quilt.

Center medallion fabric requirements and cutting

Yardages are based on 42" wide fabric. All strips are cut across the width of the fabric.

The following yardage requirements and cutting instructions are for the center medallion *only.*

Wine ¼ yd

Cut 2 strips 3½" x 42"
From these, cut
2 pieces 3½" x 12½"
6 pieces 3½" x 6½"
4 pieces 3½" x 3½"

Turquoise Green ¼ yd

Cut 1 strip 6½" x 42"
From this, cut 5 squares 6½" x 6½"
(Set aside 4 squares for the fifth border.)

Black ⅞ yd

Center Medallion

Cut 3 strips 3½" x 42"
From these, cut 4 pieces 3½" x 9½"
8 pieces 3½" x 6½"
(Set aside 4 strips for the first border.)
4 pieces 3½" x 3½"

Inner Spacing Border

Cut 2 strips 1½" x 42"
From these, cut
2 pieces 1½" x 20½"
2 pieces 1½" x 18½"

Outer Spacing Border

Cut 3 strips 2½" x 42"
From these, cut
2 strips 2½" x 24½"
2 strips 2½" x 20½"

Batting 31" x 31"

Backing 1 yd (31" x 31")

Binding ⅜ yd (3 strips 2½" x 42")

Piecing the Center Medallion

Fig. 1. Center medallion. Finished size: 24½" x 24½".

1. From your black and wine rectangles and squares, piece two each of units A–D shown in figure 2 using the corner-square technique. (See Tips on Piecing Corner-Square Units on page 9). Press the seam allowance toward the dark fabric.

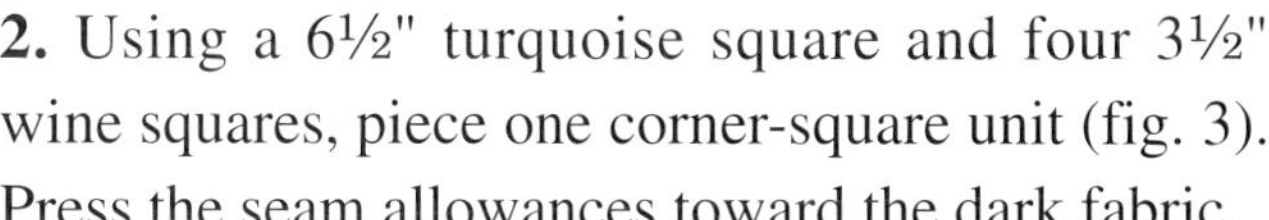

2. Using a 6½" turquoise square and four 3½" wine squares, piece one corner-square unit (fig. 3). Press the seam allowances toward the dark fabric.

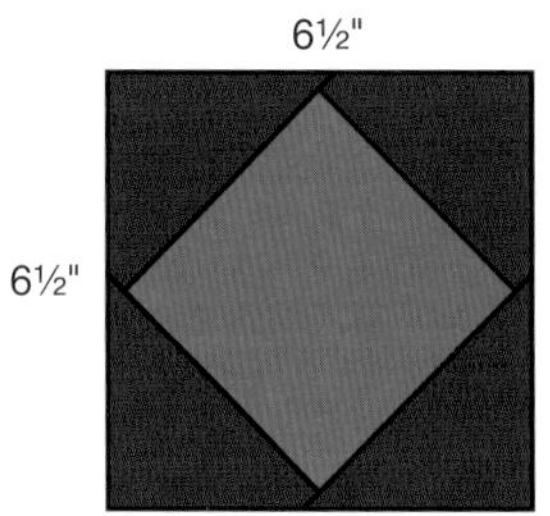

Fig. 3. Make one unit.

3. To finish the center medallion block, sew the units from steps 1 and 2 according to the quilt assembly diagram (fig. 4) on page 18.

4. Add the black spacing-border strips, as shown in the assembly diagram. If you plan to stop here, secure the batting and backing to the quilt top, quilt as desired, and add the binding.

5. If you plan to add the first pieced border, your quilt top must measure 24½" x 24½".

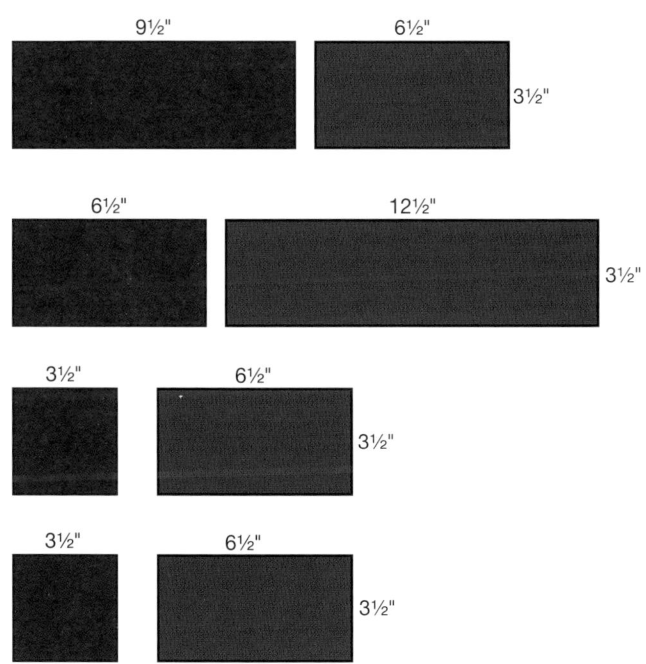

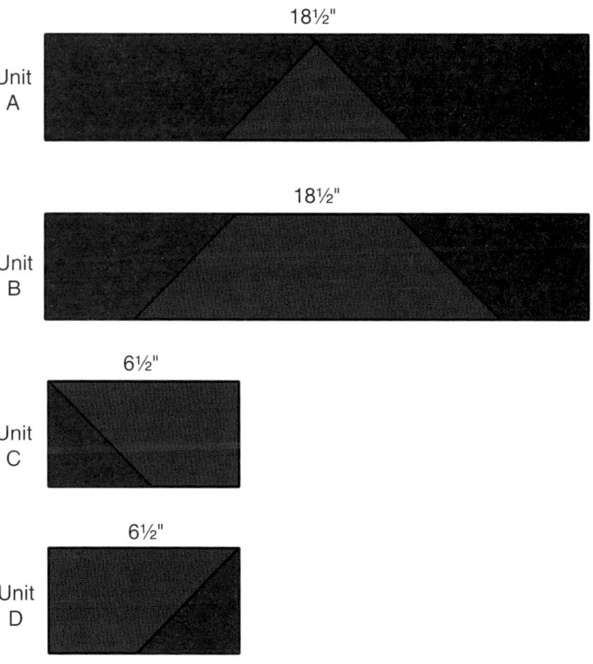

Fig. 2. Make two of each unit.

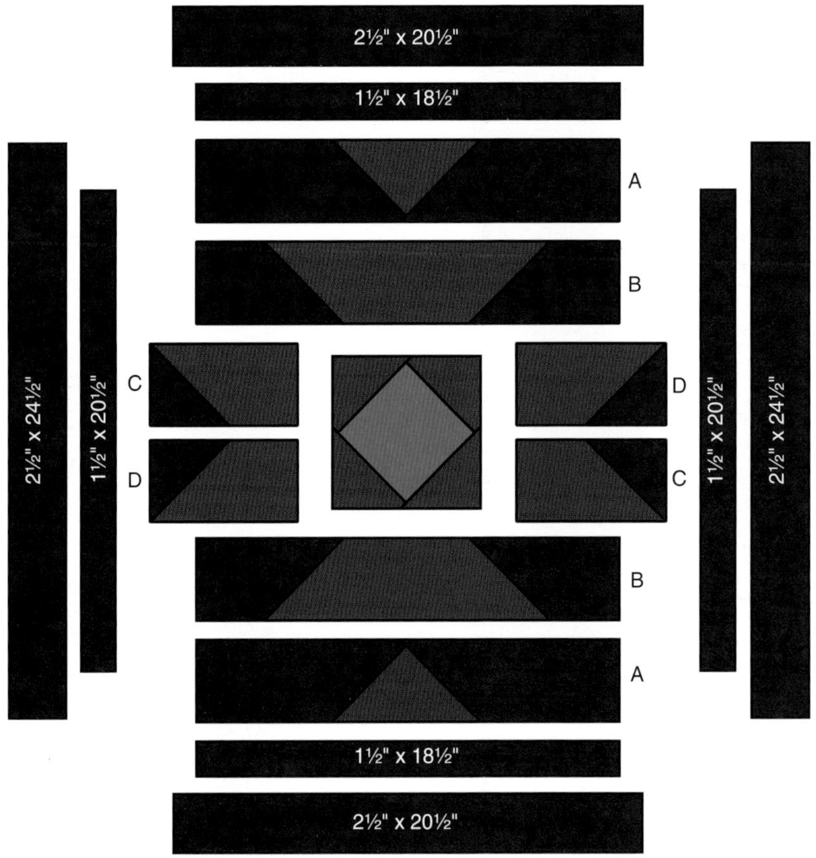

Fig. 4. Center medallion assembly

First Pieced Border

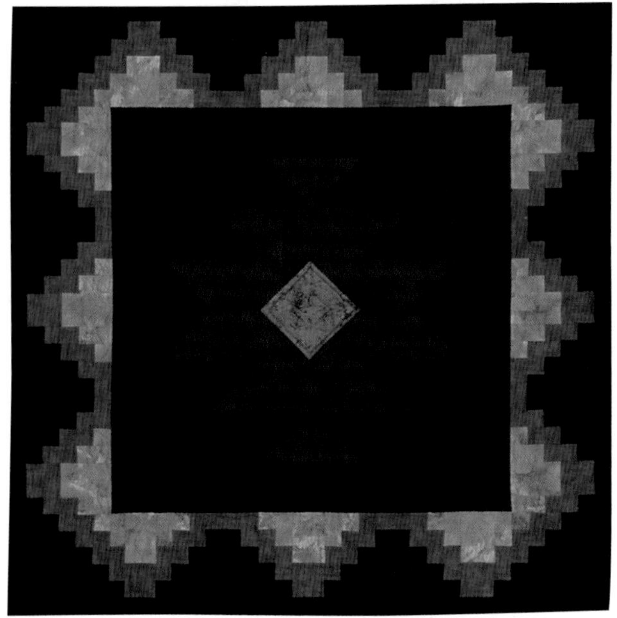

Fig. 5. First pieced border. Finished size: 40½" x 40½".

Fabric requirements and cutting

The following yardage requirements and cutting instructions are for the first pieced border *only*. These yardage requirements should be added to the amounts given for the center medallion. Yardages are based on 42" wide fabric. All strips are cut across the width of the fabric.

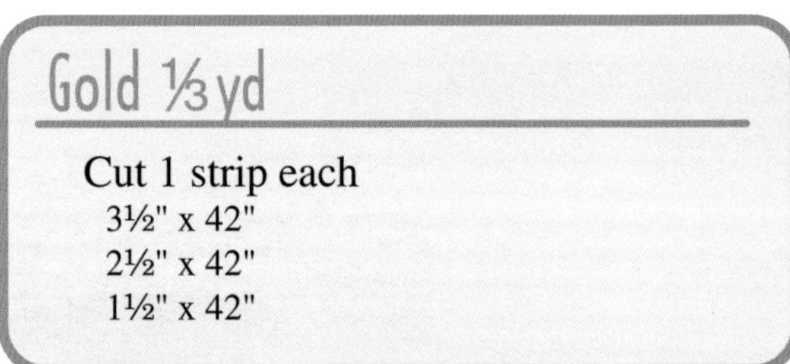

Gold ⅓ yd

Cut 1 strip each
- 3½" x 42"
- 2½" x 42"
- 1½" x 42"

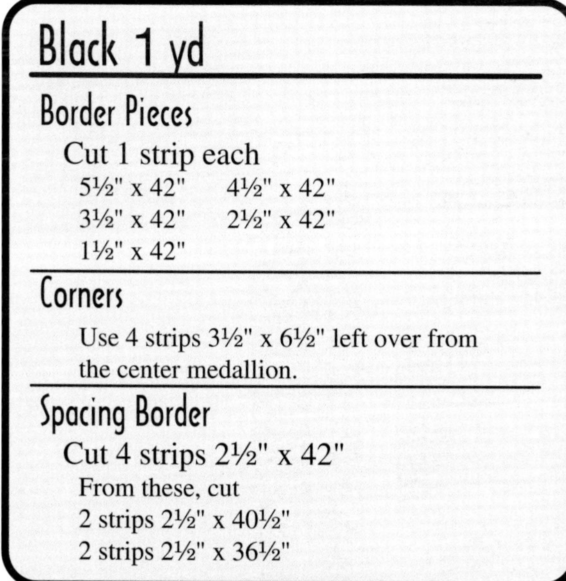

Black 1 yd

Border Pieces

Cut 1 strip each

5½" x 42"   4½" x 42"
3½" x 42"   2½" x 42"
1½" x 42"

Corners

Use 4 strips 3½" x 6½" left over from the center medallion.

Spacing Border

Cut 4 strips 2½" x 42"

From these, cut
2 strips 2½" x 40½"
2 strips 2½" x 36½"

Turquoise Blue ½ yd

Cut 4 strips 2½" x 42"
Cut 1 strip 1½" x 42"

Batting 46" x 46"

Backing 2¾ yd (2 lengths 46", pieced vertically)

Binding ½ yd (5 strips 2½" x 42")

Piecing the first border

1. Start with the A segments. Piece the 42" black, gold, and turquoise blue strip-sets shown in figure 6. (See Tips on Strip Piecing on page 10). Press the seam allowances in one direction. Cut the strip-set into 24 segments 1½" wide. Set these segments aside for now.

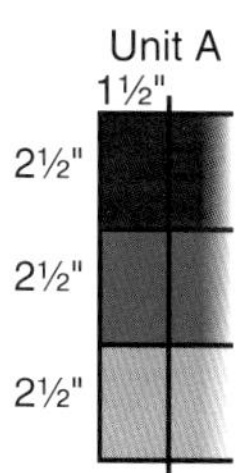

Fig. 6. Piece a 42" strip-set and cut 24 segments.

2. Referring to the diagrams in figure 7, piece the 42" strip-sets for segments B through F. Press the seam allowances in one direction, and cut the segments as shown in the diagrams.

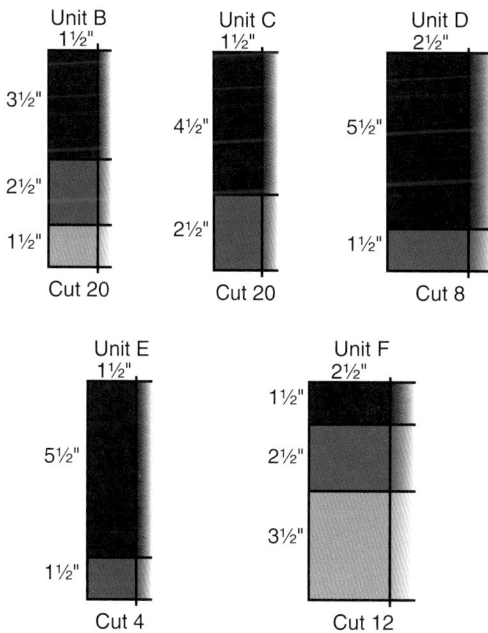

Fig. 7. Piece 42" strip-sets and cut segments B through F.

3. Assemble four border units (fig. 8). Press the seam allowances in one direction.

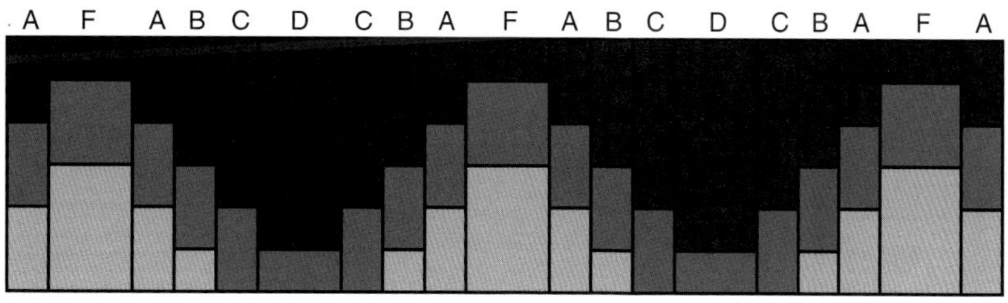

Fig. 8. Use segments A through F to assemble border units.

4. Make two corner Y units and two corner YR units (fig. 9). Press the seam allowances in one direction.

5. Sew the first two border units to the top and bottom of your quilt, then add your corner units to the remaining two border units and sew them to your quilt according to the assembly diagram in figure 10.

6. Sew your spacing-border strips to the lengths shown in the assembly diagram.

7. If you plan to stop here, secure the batting and backing to the quilt top, quilt as desired, and add the binding. If you plan to add the second pieced border, your quilt top must measure 40½" x 40½".

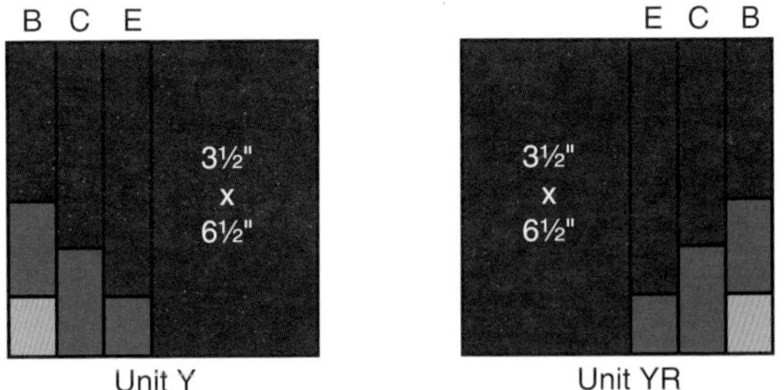

Fig. 9. Make two each of corner units Y and YR.

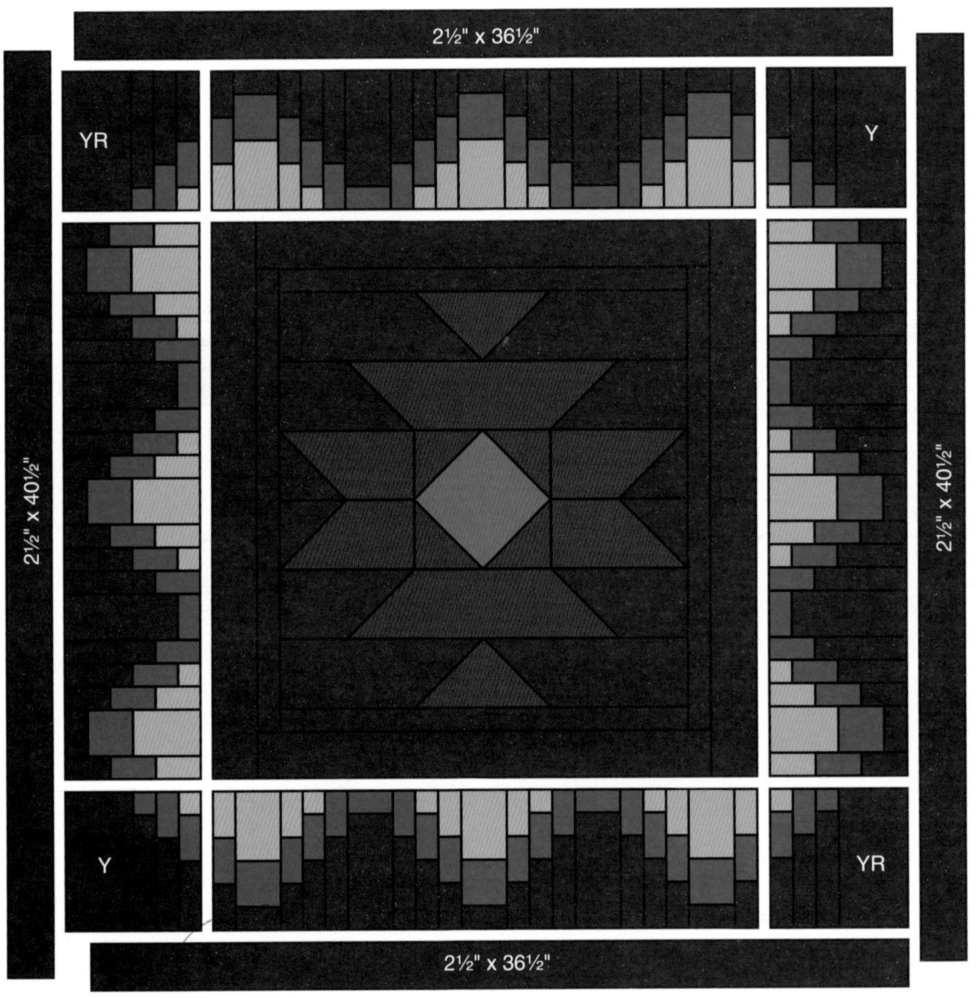

Fig. 10. First pieced-border assembly

Second Pieced Border

Fig. 11. Second pieced border. Finished size: 52½" x 52½".

Fabric requirements and cutting

The following yardage requirements and cutting instructions are for the second pieced border *only*. These yardage requirements should be added to the amounts given for the center medallion and first pieced border. Yardages are based on 42" wide fabric. All strips are cut across the width of the fabric.

Black 1½ yd

Border Pieces
Cut 10 strips 2½" x 42"
From these, cut 160 squares 2½" x 2½"

Corner Units
Cut 1 strip 4⅞" x 42"
From this, cut 2 squares 4⅞" x 4⅞"

Spacing Border
Cut 6 strips 2½" x 42"

Olive Green 1 yd

Border Pieces
Cut 5 strips 4½" x 42"
From these, cut 80 strips 2½" x 4½"

Corner Units
Cut 1 strip 4⅞" x 42"
From this, cut 2 squares 4⅞" x 4⅞"

Batting 58" x 58"
Backing 3⅓ yd (2 lengths 58", pieced vertically)
Binding ½ yd (6 strips 2½" x 42")

Piecing the second border

1. Piece black 2½" squares and green 2½" x 4½" rectangles to make 40 of each corner-square unit (fig. 12a). Press the seam allowances toward the dark fabric. Join these into 40 of the pairs shown in figure 12b.

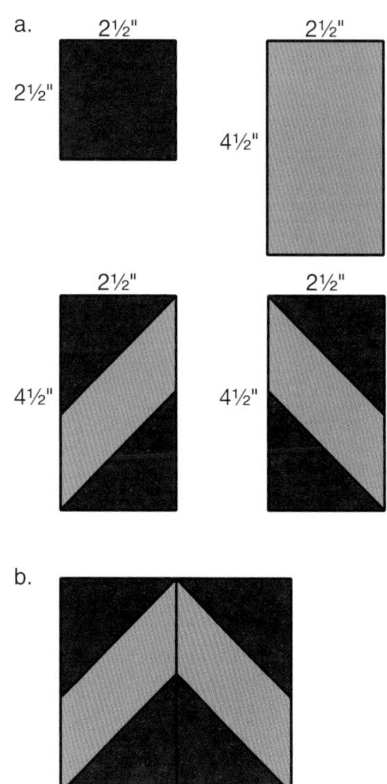

Fig. 12. Piece 40 of each corner-square unit (a), and sew pairs together (b).

2. Assemble four pieced-border units (fig. 13).

Fig.13. Border assembly. Make four.

3. For the corner units, use the black and the green 4⅞" squares to make four half-square triangle units. (See Tips on Piecing Half-Square Triangles on page 8.) Sew these to two pieced-border units as shown in figure 14.

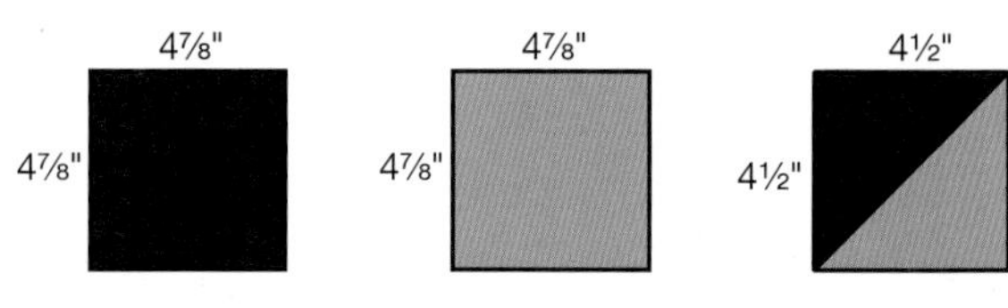

Fig. 14. Sew corner units to pieced-border units. Make two.

4. Sew your border units to your quilt according to the quilt assembly diagram in figure 15.

5. Using diagonal seams, join the six black spacing-border strips to form one long strip. Cut and sew your black spacing border strips as shown in the assembly diagram.

6. If you plan to stop here, secure the batting and backing to the quilt top, quilt as desired, and add the binding. If you plan to add the third pieced border, your quilt top must measure 52½" x 52½".

Fig. 15. Second pieced border assembly

Third Pieced Border

Fig. 16. Third pieced border. Finished size: 68½" x 68½".

Fabric requirements and cutting

The following yardage requirements and cutting instructions are for the third pieced border *only*. These yardage requirements should be added to the amounts given for the center medallion and the first and second pieced borders. Yardages are based on 42" wide fabric. All strips are cut across the width of the fabric.

Red 1 yd

Pieced Border
- Cut 2 strips 6½" x 42"
  - From these, cut 24 strips 6½" x 2½"
- Cut 1 strip 4½" x 42"
  - From this, cut 8 squares 4½" x 4½"
- Cut 3 strips 2½" x 42"

Black 1¾ yd

Pieced Border
- Cut 2 strips 6½" x 42"
  - From these, cut
  - 16 strips 6½" x 2½"
  - 24 strips 6½" x 1½"
- Cut 1 strip 4½" x 42"
  - From this, cut 16 strips 4½" x 1½"
- Cut 8 strips 2½" x 42"
  - From these, cut 2 strips into
  - 32 squares 2½" x 2½"
  - (Set aside 6 strips for strip-sets.)

Spacing Border
- Cut 7 strips 2½" x 42"

Batting 74" x 74"

Backing 4⅓ yd (2 lengths 74", pieced horizontally)

Binding ⅝ yd (8 strips 2½" x 42")

Piecing the third border

1. Piece three black and red strip-sets 42" long, as shown in figure 17. (See Tips on Strip Piecing on page 10). Press the seam allowances in the same direction. Cut 48 segments 2½" wide.

2. With the segments from step 1 and red strips shown in figure 18, assemble 24 A units.

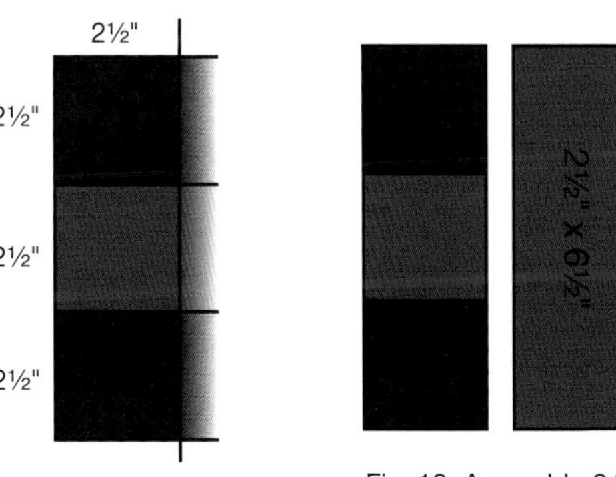

Fig. 17. Make three strip-sets and cut 48 segments.

Fig. 18. Assemble 24 A units.

3. With the 4½" red squares and the 2½" black squares piece eight corner-square units (fig. 19). (See Tips on Piecing Corner Square Units on page 9.) Use 1½" wide black strips to assemble eight B units, as shown.

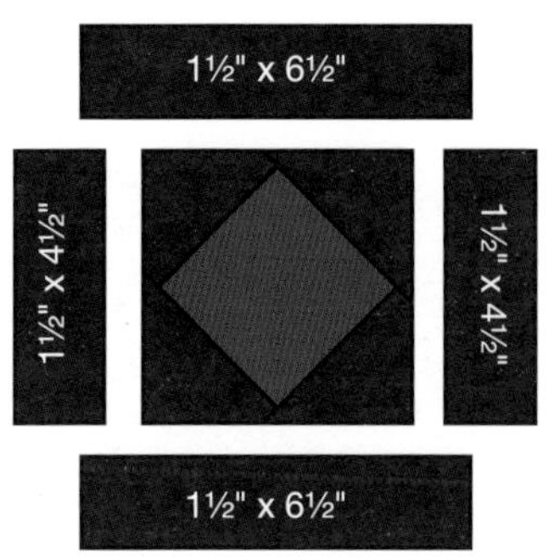

Fig. 19. Make eight B units.

4. Assemble four border units beginning and ending with a narrow 1½" black strip, as shown in figure 20.

5. Add a B unit to each end of two of the border units (fig. 21) for the right- and left-side pieced borders.

6. Sew your border units to your quilt according to the assembly diagram in figure 22.

7. Using diagonal seams, join the seven black spacing-border strips to form one long strip. Cut and sew your black spacing border strips as shown in the quilt assembly diagram.

8. If you plan to stop here, secure the batting and backing to the quilt top, quilt as desired, and add the binding. If you plan to add the fourth pieced border, your quilt top must measure 68½" x 68½".

Fig. 22. Third pieced border assembly

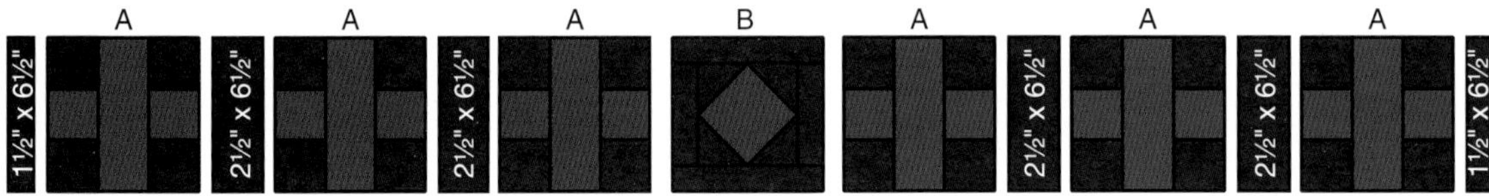

Fig. 20. Assemble four pieced border units.

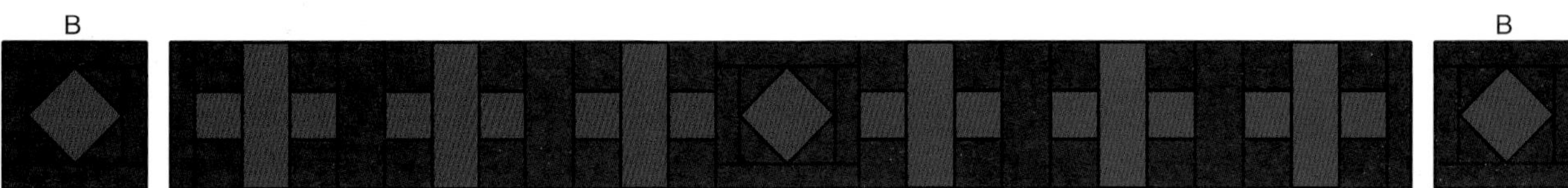

Fig. 21. Add B units to make the corners for the third pieced border.

Fourth Pieced Border

Fig. 23. Fourth pieced border. Finished size: 80½" x 80½".

Fabric requirements and cutting

The following yardage requirements and cutting instructions are for the fourth pieced border *only*. These yardage requirements should be added to the amounts given for the center medallion and the first, second, and third pieced borders. Yardages are based on 42" wide fabric. All strips are cut across the width of the fabric.

Black 2 yd

Pieced Border

Cut 2 strips 1½" x 42"

Cut 6 strips 2½" x 42"

From these, cut 96 squares 2½" x 2½"

Cut 6 strips 4½" x 42"

From these, cut 76 strips 2½" x 4½"

4 squares 4½" x 4½"

Spacing Border

Cut 9 strips 2½" x 42"

Eggplant 1 yd

Pieced Border

Cut 3 strips 4½" x 42"

From these, cut 48 strips 2½" x 4½"

Cut 6 strips 2½" x 42"

From these, cut 96 squares 2½" x 2½"

Melon ⅛ yd

Cut 1 strip 2½" x 42"

Batting 86" x 86"

Backing 5 yd

(2 lengths 86" long, pieced horizontally)

Binding ¾ yd (9 strips 2½" x 42")

Piecing the fourth border

1. Referring to figure 24, piece one black and melon strip-set 42" long. Press the seam allowances in the same direction. Cut 24 segments 1½" wide.

2. Using the eggplant and black 2½" x 4½" rectangles and the eggplant and black 2½" squares, sew 48 corner-square A units and 48 corner-square B units (fig. 25).

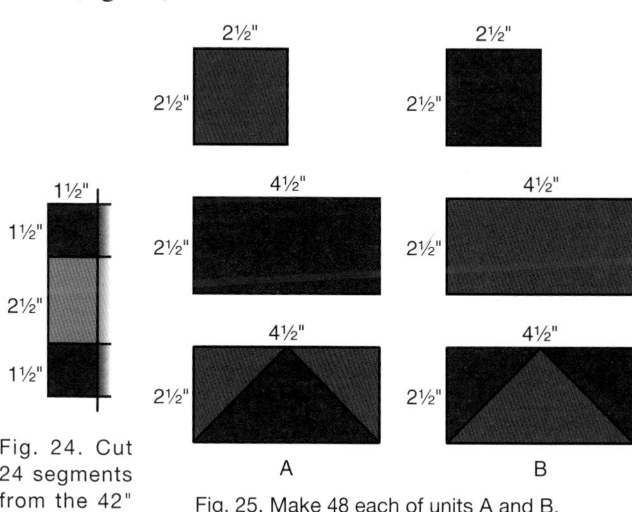

Fig. 24. Cut 24 segments from the 42" strip set.

Fig. 25. Make 48 each of units A and B.

3. Use the segments from step 1 and the corner-square units from step 2 to assemble 24 units, as shown in figure 26.

4. Using the 2½" x 4½" black strips and the units pieced in step 3, sew four border units (fig. 27) beginning and ending with a black strip.

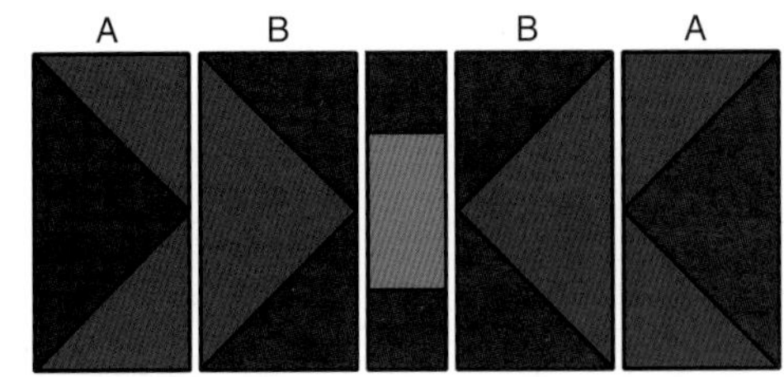

Fig. 26. Make 24 units.

Fig. 27. Assemble four pieced border units.

5. Sew two of the border units to the top and bottom of the quilt. Add a 4½" black square to each end of the remaining two border units and sew them to the sides of the quilt according to the assembly diagram in figure 28.

6. Using diagonal seams, join the nine black spacing-border strips to form one long strip. Cut and sew your spacing-border strips as shown in the assembly diagram.

7. If you plan to stop here, secure the batting and backing to the quilt top, quilt as desired, and add the binding. If you plan to add the fifth pieced border, your quilt top must measure 80½" x 80½".

Fig. 28. Fourth pieced-border assembly

Fifth Pieced Border

Fig. 29. The fifth border completes your MIDNIGHT IN SANTA FE quilt.

Fabric requirements and cutting

The following yardage requirements and cutting instructions are for the fifth pieced border *only*. These yardage requirements should be added to the amounts given for the center medallion and the first, second, third, and fourth pieced borders. Yardages are based on 42" wide fabric. All strips are cut across the width of the fabric.

Black 1¾ yd

Pieced Border

Cut 5 strips 5½" x 42"
From these, cut
8 strips 4½" x 5½"
64 strips 2½" x 5½"
Cut 9 strips 1½" x 42"
Cut 5 strips 2½" x 42"
From these, cut 80 squares 2½" x 2½"

Border Corners

Cut 1 strip 4½" x 42"
From this, cut 4 squares 4½" x 4½"

Turquoise Green 2½ yd

Pieced Border

Cut 5 strips 5½" x 42"
From these, cut 80 strips 2½" x 5½"
Cut 4 strips 2½" x 42"
From these, cut 64 squares 2½" x 2½"
Cut 1 strips 4½" x 42"
From this, cut 8 squares 4½" x 4½"

Border Corners

Use the 4 squares 6½" x 6½" reserved from the center medallion.

Outer Border

Cut 5 strips 4½" x 42"
Cut 6 strips 2½" x 42"

Batting 102" x 106"

Backing 9 yd
(3 lengths 102", pieced horizontally)

Binding ¾ yd (10 strips 2½" x 42")

Piecing the fifth border

1. Use the 2½" x 5½" turquoise green rectangles and the 2½" black squares to piece 40 of each corner-square shown in figure 30. Press the seam allowances open. Join the corner squares to make 40 A units.

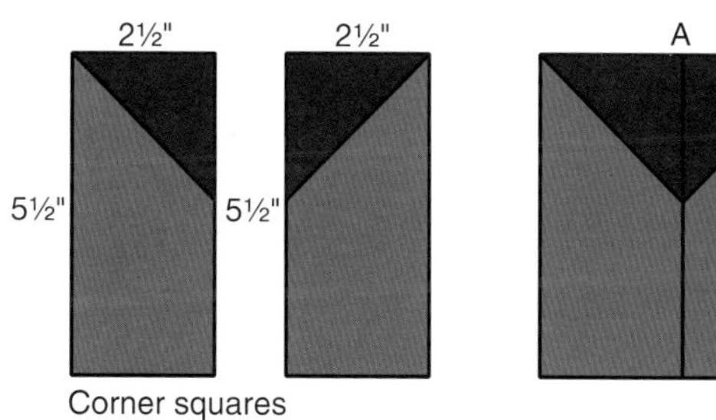

Fig. 30. Make 40 A units.

2. Use the 2½" x 5½" black rectangles and the 2½" turquoise green squares to piece 32 of each corner-square shown in figure 31. Press the seam allowances open. Join the corner squares to make 32 B units.

3. Use the 4½" x 5½" black rectangles and the 4½" turquoise green squares to picce four of each corner-square unit shown in figure 32. Press the seam allowances open. Join the corner squares to make four C units.

4. Using diagonal seams, join the nine black 1½" strips to form one long strip. Cut into four strips 1½" x 80½". Assemble four border units as shown in figure 33. Press the seam allowances toward the black.

5. Use the 6½" turquoise green squares and the 4½" black squares to piece four corner-square units, as shown in figure 34. Sew your border units and corner-square units to your quilt according to the assembly diagram on page 29.

6. Using diagonal seams, join the five turquoise green 4½" strips to form one long strip. Cut and sew these strips to the top and bottom of your quilt top, as shown in the assembly diagram.

7. Using diagonal seams, join the six turquoise green 2½" strips to form one long strip. Cut and sew these strips to each side of your quilt top, as shown in the assembly diagram. Secure the batting and backing to the quilt top, quilt as desired, and add the binding.

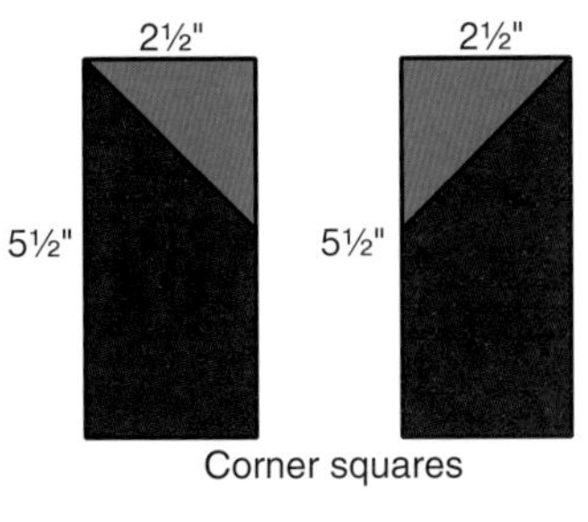

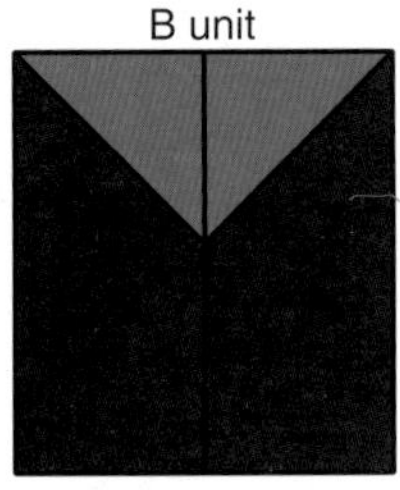

Fig. 31. Make 32 B units.

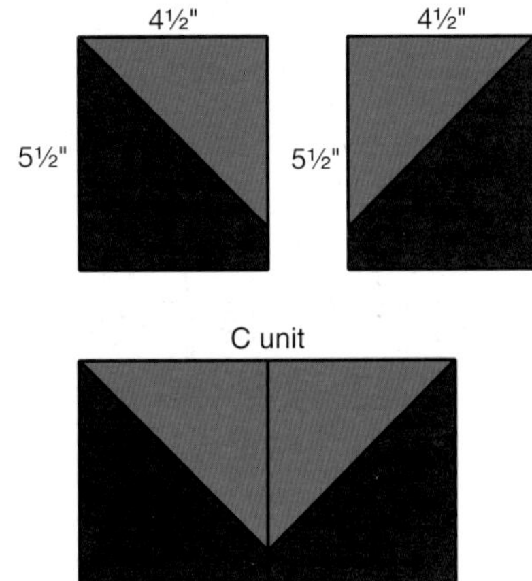

Fig. 32. Make four C units.

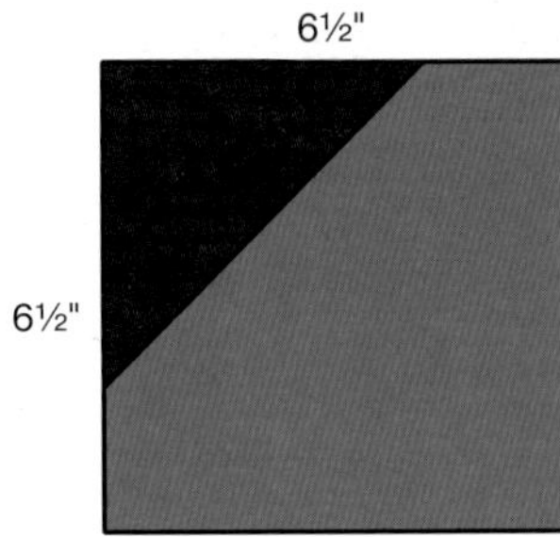

Fig. 34. Make four corner units.

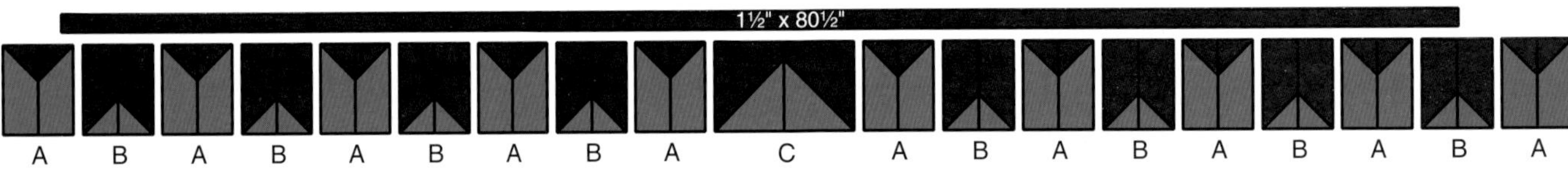

Fig. 33. Make four border units.

Fig. 35. Fifth pieced border assembly

Southwest Medallion Wallhanging

Pieced by Jan Hightower, Roswell, New Mexico. Machine quilted by Glenda Raby, Roswell, New Mexico.

Jemez Memories

Pieced by Alexis Swoboda, Roswell, New Mexico. Machine quilted by Richard Larson, Plano, Texas.

Eye Dazzler

EYE DAZZLER, 72" x 80". Made by the author. Quilted by Richard Larson, Plano, Texas.

The Eye Dazzler weavings were popular in the late 1890s. These gaudy Navajo weavings were strongly influenced by the Rio Grande weavings. The quilt block pattern that I used to create this "eye dazzler" was a variation of the traditional Delectable Mountain quilt block. For another eye dazzling quilt, try using scraps where I used the batik prints.

Fabric requirements and cutting

Yardages are based on 42" wide fabric. All strips are cut across the width of the fabric.

Dark Brown 4⅝ yd

Pieced Blocks

Cut 9 strips 8⅞" x 42"

From these, cut 36 squares 8⅞" x 8⅞"
Then cut diagonally into 72 triangles.

Cut 11 strips 2⅞" x 42"

From these, cut 144 squares 2⅞" x 2⅞"

Cut 5 strips 2½" x 42"

From these, cut 72 squares 2½" x 2½"

Outer Border

Cut 8 strips 3½" x 42"

Batik Print 2⅝ yd

Pieced Blocks

Cut 5 strips 4⅞" x 42"

From these, cut 36 squares 4⅞" x 4⅞"
Then cut diagonally into 72 triangles.

Cut 16 strips 2⅞" x 42"

From these, cut 216 squares 2⅞" x 2⅞"
Then cut 72 of these squares diagonally into 144 triangles.

Inner Border

Cut 8 strips 1½" x 42"

Batting 78" x 86"

Backing 5 yd (2 lengths 86" pieced vertically)

Binding ⅝ yd (8 strips 2½" x 42")

Making the Eye Dazzler Block

1. Sew 144 pairs of 2⅞" dark brown and batik squares with diagonal rows of stitching. (See Tips on Piecing Half-Square Triangles on page 8.) From these, cut 288 half-square triangle units (fig. 1).

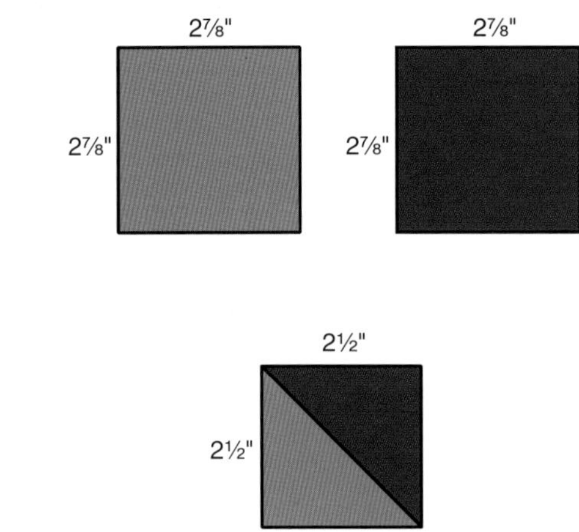

Fig. 1. Cut 288 units.

2. Using the 2½" dark brown squares, the 2⅞" batik triangles, and the 288 half-square triangle units, assemble 72 A units and 72 B units, as shown in figure 2.

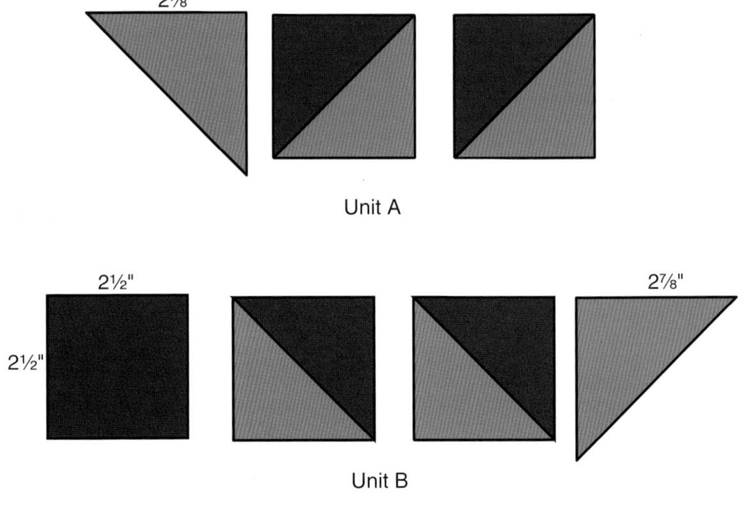

Fig. 2. Assemble 72 of each unit.

3. Using units A and B and the 4⅞" batik triangles, sew 72 triangle units (fig. 3).

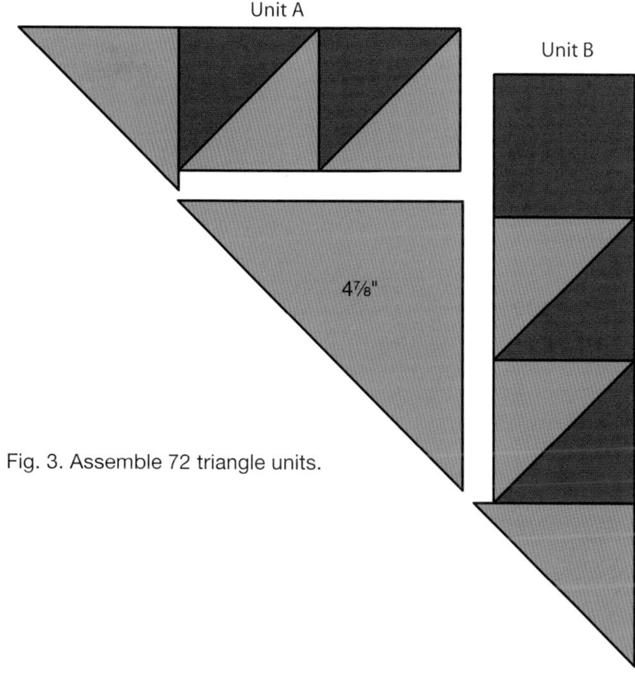

Fig. 3. Assemble 72 triangle units.

4. Use the triangle units from step 3 and the 8⅞" brown triangles to assemble 72 blocks (fig. 4). Press the seam allowances toward the dark triangles.

5. Sew the blocks into 5 X rows and 4 Y rows, as shown in figure 5.

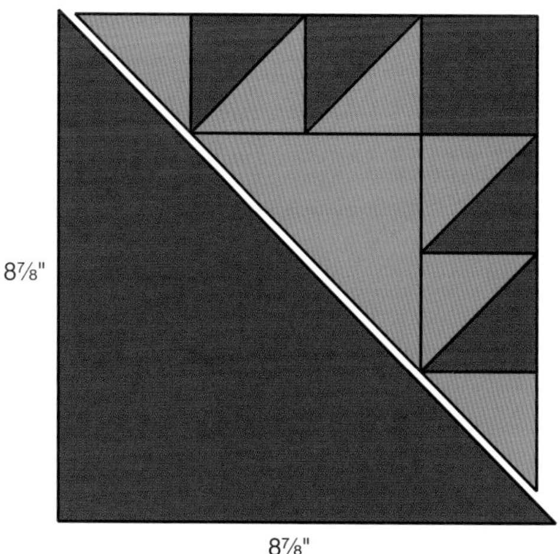

Fig. 4. EYE DAZZLER block assembly

Assembling and Finishing Your Quilt

1. Join rows according to the quilt assembly diagram on page 36. Press the seam allowances in one direction.

2. Using diagonal seams, sew the eight batik inner border strips together to form one long strip. Cut two strips 1½" x 64½". Sew these strips to the top and bottom edges of the quilt top. Press the seam allowances outward. Cut two strips 1½" x 74½". Sew these strips to each side of the quilt top, and press seam allowances outward.

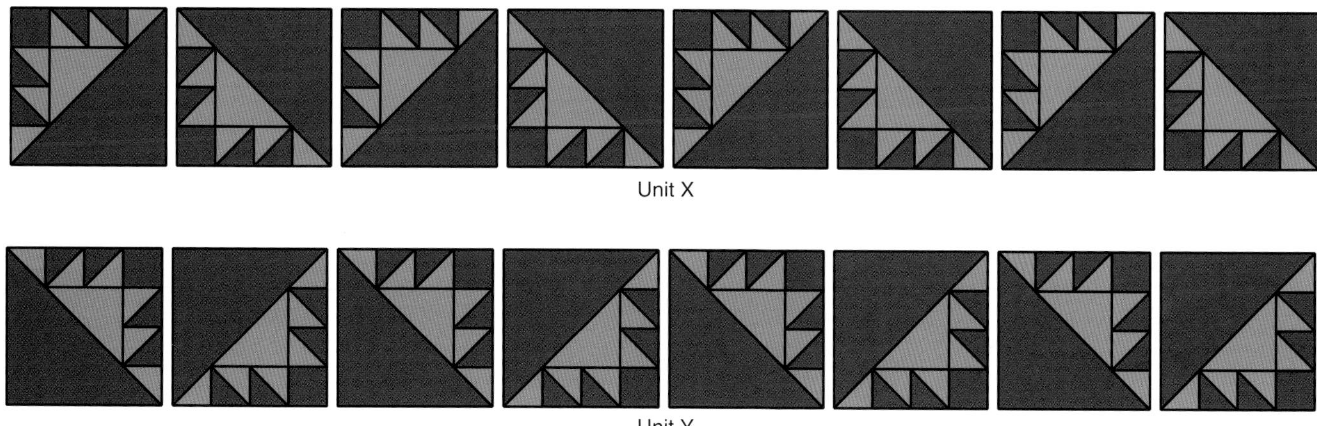

Fig. 5. Assemble rows X and Y.

4. Using diagonal seams, sew the brown outer border strips together to form one long strip. From this long strip, cut two strips 3½" x 66½". Sew these strips to the top and bottom edges of the quilt top. Press the seam allowances outward. Cut two strips 3½" x 80½". Sew these strips to each side of the quilt top, and press seam allowances outward.

5. Layer the quilt top, batting and backing. Baste the layers together. Quilt as desired. Bind the edges to finish.

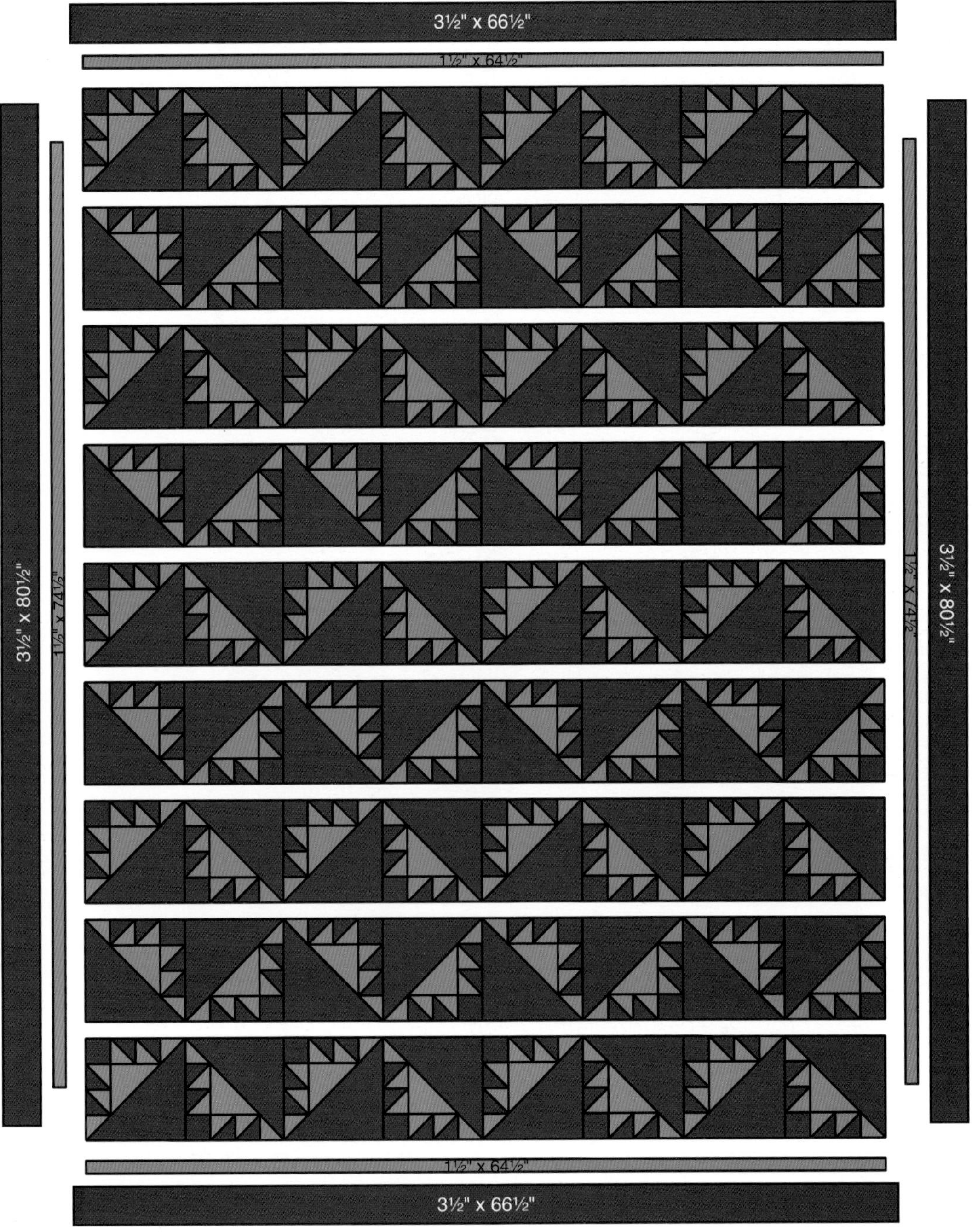

Fig. 6. EYE DAZZLER quilt assembly

Bright Latilla

BRIGHT LATILLA, 42" x 54". Made by the author.

Pueblo floors are packed earth. The ceilings are made by embedding large poles in the tops of the walls to span the room. These poles, called vigas, are large tree trunks. Latillas are small branches that are placed across the vigas to form the ceiling. These small branches can be peeled and used in their natural color or painted for additional color. Latillas are also used in furniture design.

As a quilt artist, sometimes inspiration comes from rather odd places. The ceiling in a friend's house was the inspiration for this quilt. This is a vertical-row quilt that can be created with your scraps. The throw size BRIGHT LATILLA *quilt is great for over the back of a chair.*

Fabric requirements and cutting

Yardages are based on 42" wide fabric. All strips are cut across the width of the fabric.

Muslin 1⅝ yd

Foundation Pieces
4 strips 9" x 53"
(cut from the length of the fabric)

Bright Scraps 2¾ yd

Latilla Pieces
Cut approximately 130 strips
13" long in a variety of widths from 1" to 2½"

Dark Brown ¾ yd

Sashing and Borders
9 strips 2½" x 42"

Batting 48" x 62"
Backing 2⅞ yd
(2 lengths 48" long, pieced horizontally)
Binding ½ yd (6 strips 2½" x 42")

Foundation Piecing the Latilla Panels

1. Mark two muslin strips with 60-degree stitching guides slanting toward the left every 4" to 6". Mark two muslin strips with 60-degree stitching guides slanting toward the right every 4" to 6" (fig. 1).

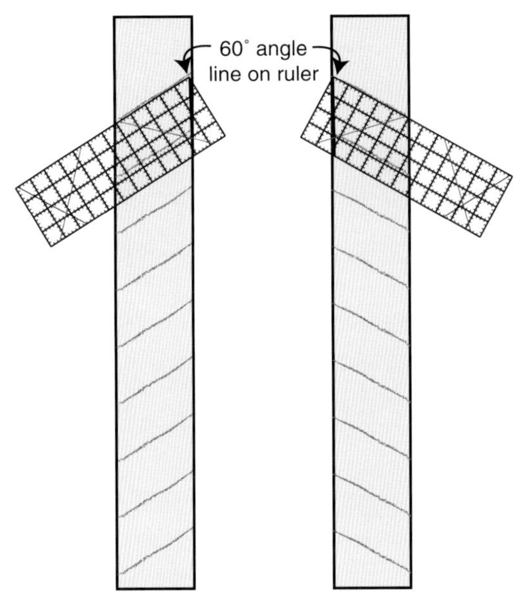

Fig. 1. Mark right- and left-slanting stitching guides.

2. You will sew strips to the muslin bases, using the flip-and-sew technique and following your right- and left-slanting stitching guides. Place the first strip on the corner of a muslin base and pin the strip in place. Position the next strip right-side down, aligning the raw edges of the strips. Sew the strips to the muslin base, using a ¼" seam allowance (fig. 2).

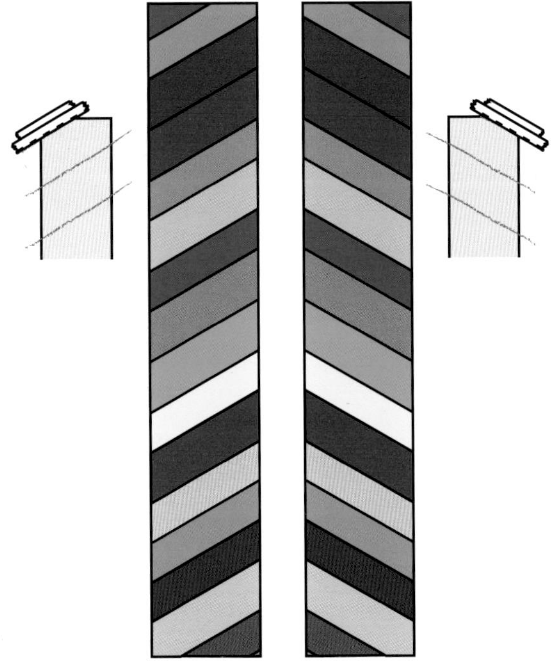

Fig. 2. Flip and sew the latilla strips, keeping them aligned with the stitching guides.

3. Flip the second strip over and press. Pin a new strip right-side down and repeat the sew-and-flip process to cover the entire length of the muslin base.

4. Trim each latilla panel to measure 8½" x 50½".

Assembling and Finishing Your Quilt

1. Using diagonal seams, sew nine dark brown strips 2½" x 42" together to form one long strip. Cut five sashing strips 2½" x 50½".

2. Sew your latilla panels and sashing strips together, according to the quilt assembly diagram in figure 3. Press the seam allowances toward the sashing strips.

3. Cut two strips 2½" x 42½". Sew these strips to the top and bottom edges of the quilt top. Press the seam allowances outward.

4. Layer the quilt top, batting, and backing. Baste the layers together and quilt as desired. Bind the edges to finish the quilt.

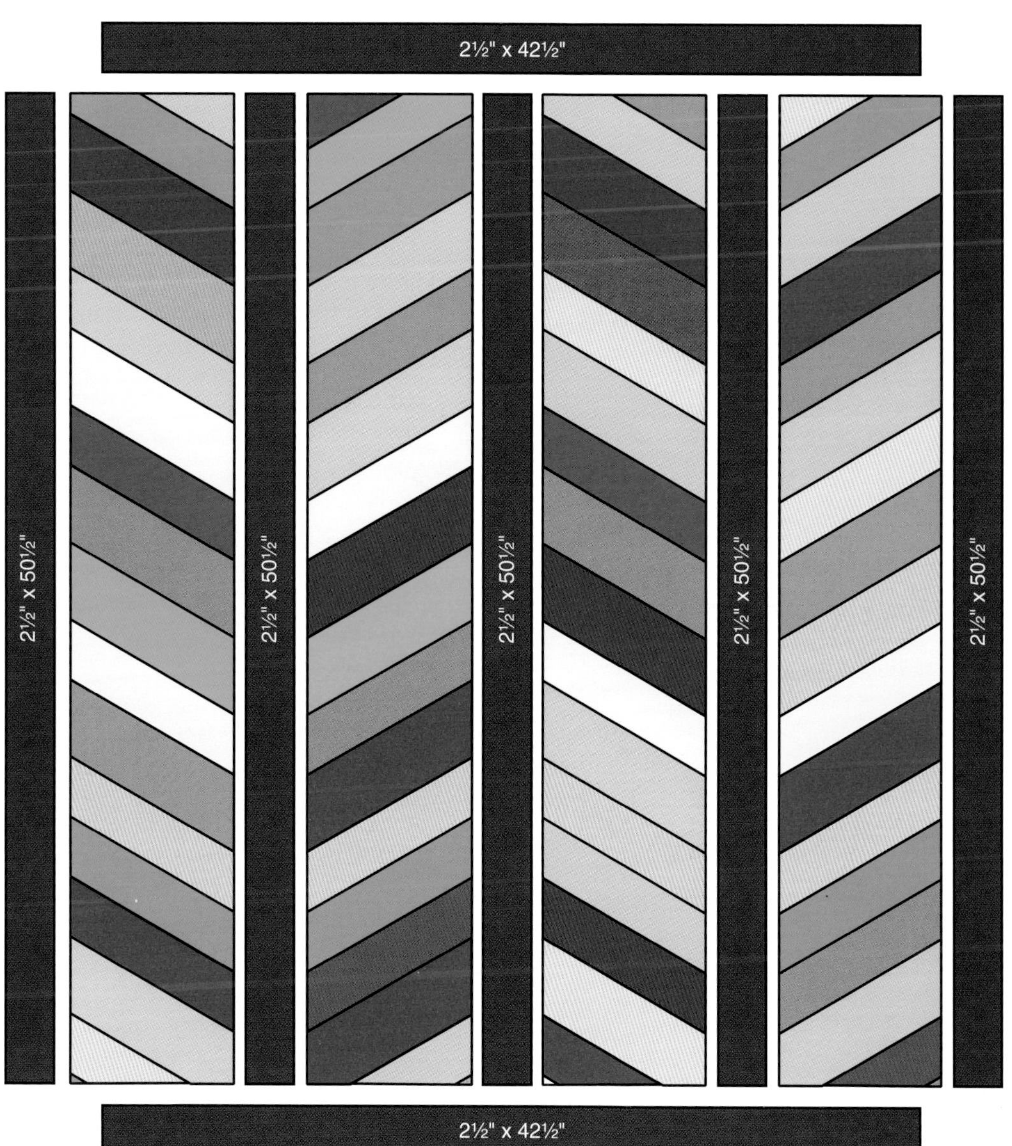

FIG. 3. BRIGHT LATILLA quilt assembly

Natural Latilla

NATURAL LATILLA, 86" x 100". Pieced by the author and machine quilted by Phyllis Kent, Los Lunas, New Mexico.

NATURAL LATILLA is my original version of a latilla quilt. I used over 70 different fabrics from my stash for the large quilt. Follow the general instructions for piecing a latilla panel.

Fabric requirements and cutting

Yardages are based on 42" wide fabric. All strips are cut across the width of the fabric.

Earth-Tone Scraps 9 yd

Latilla Pieces

Cut approximately 540 strips 13" long in a variety of widths from 1" to 2½"

Muslin 5½ yd

Foundation Pieces

8 strips 9" x 94"
(cut from the length of the fabric)

Beige Speckle 2⅝ yd

Sashing

Cut 17 strips 2½" x 42"

Top and Bottom Borders

Cut 10 strips 4½" x 42"

Batting 92" x 106"

Backing 8¼ yd
(3 lengths 94" long, pieced horizontally)

Binding ¾ yd (10 strips 2½" x 42")

Making Natural Latilla

1. Mark four muslin strips with 60-degree stitching guides slanting toward the left every 4" to 6". Mark four muslin strips with 60-degree stitching guides slanting toward the right every 4" to 6" (fig. 1, page 36).

2. Sew the strips to the muslin bases, using the flip-and-sew technique, as shown in figure 2 on page 36.

3. Trim each latilla panel to measure 8½" x 92½".

4. Using diagonal seams, sew 17 beige-speckle sashing strips together to form one long strip. Cut seven sashing strips 2½" x 92½". Sew the sashing strips and latilla panels together according to the Natural Latilla assembly diagram (fig. 4, page 40). Press the seam allowances toward the sashing strips.

5. Using diagonal seams, sew 10 beige-speckle border strips together to form one long strip. Cut two strips 4½" x 92½". Sew them to the left and right sides of the quilt, according the assembly diagram. Press the seam allowances outward.

6. Cut two strips 4½" x 86½". Sew them to the top and bottom edges of the quilt, according to the assembly diagram. Press the seam allowances outward.

7. Layer the quilt top, batting, and backing. Baste the layers together and quilt as desired. Bind the edges to finish the quilt.

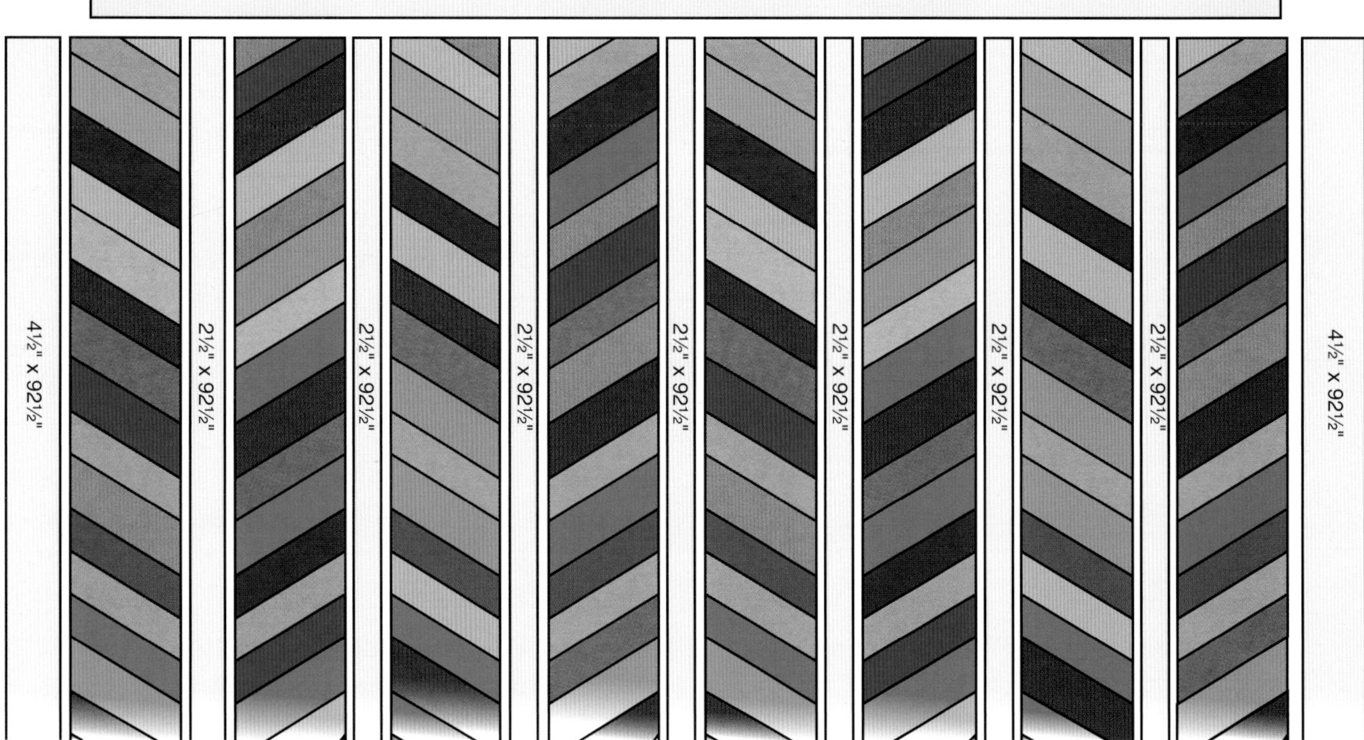

Fig. 4. NATURAL LATILLA quilt assembly

Finding Inspiration

The earthy wood tones in aspen and cedar branches inspired my fabric choices as set together in the NATURAL LATILLA quilt. I worked with a color palette that included several shades of beiges, tans, browns, golds, grays, and rusts. The colors used in BRIGHT LATILLA were inspired by the brightly painted branches that are commonly used in a unique style of furniture.

Pueblo Cross

PUEBLO CROSS, 48" x 48". Made by Cheryl Gustafson, Albuquerque, New Mexico. Machine quilted by the author.

This is a very unique weaving design. Cross designs were popular in Navajo weavings after 1865. The cross designs used in weavings were influenced by the Plains Indian beadwork patterns.

Fabric requirements and cutting

Yardages are based on 42" wide fabric. All strips are cut across the width of the fabric.

Gold 1¼ yd

Corner Units

Cut 3 strips 8" x 42"
From these, cut 2 strips 8" x 2½"
and 1 strip each

8" x 14½"	8" x 9½"	8" x 5½"
8" x 13½"	8" x 8½"	8" x 4½"
8" x 12½"	8" x 7½"	8" x 3½"
8" x 11½"	8" x 6½"	8" x 1½"
8" x 10½"		

Set aside 1 strip 8" x 2½" for outer crosses.

Outer Crosses

Cut 1 strip each
6½" x 42"
4½" x 42"

Red ¾ yd

Corner Units

Cut 2 strips 8" x 42"
From these, cut 2 strips 8" x 9½"
and 1 strip each

8" x 10½"	8" x 6½"	8" x 3½"
8" x 8½"	8" x 5½"	8" x 2½"
8" x 7½"	8" x 4½"	8" x 1½"

Set aside 1 strip 8" x 9½" for outer crosses.

Outer Crosses

Cut 1 strip 1½" x 42"

Center Cross

Cut 1 strip 1½" x 42"
From this, cut 1 strip 1½" x 9½"
and 2 strips 1½" x 4½"

Cream or White ⅝ yd

Corner Units

Cut 2 strips 8" x 42"
From these, cut
13 strips 8" x 3½"
1 strip 8" x 2½"
1 strip 8" x 1½"

Green 1⅛ yd

Corner Units

Cut 1 strip 8" x 42"
From this, cut
15 strips 8" x 2½"
1 strip 8" x 1½"

Outer Crosses

Cut 1 strip 4½" x 42"
From these, cut
4 strips 4½" x 7½"

Center Cross

Cut 1 strip 3½" x 42"
From this, cut
4 strips 3½" x 4½"
1 strip 3½" x 8"

Outer Border

5 strips 3" x 42"

Brown ⅔ yd

Corner Units

Cut 1 strip 8" x 42"
From this, cut
11 strips 8" x 2½"
2 strips 8" x 1½"
Set aside 1 strip 8" x 1½" for center cross.

Outer Crosses

Cut 2 strips 1½" x 42"
From these, cut
4 strips 1½" x 9½"
8 strips 1½" x 4½"

Inner Border

5 strips 1½" x 42"

Batting 54" x 54"

Backing 3¼ yd
(2 lengths 54", pieced vertically or horizontally)

Binding ½ yd (5 strips 2½" x 42")

Making the Corner Units

To make the corner blocks, you will sew strip sets, cut segments, and sew the mirror-image corner blocks according to the quilt diagram on page 45.

1. Start with row 1. Piece the 8" red, brown, cream, and green strip-set shown in figure 1. (See Tips on Strip Piecing on page 10.) Press the seam allowances in one direction. Cut the strip-set into four segments 1½" wide. Set these segments aside for now.

2. Referring to the diagrams in figure 2, piece the 8" strip sets for rows 2 through 16. Press the seam allowances in one direction, and cut four segments 1½" from each strip-set.

3. Referring to figure 3 on page 44, assemble two corner A units and two corner B units.

1½" 1½" 1½" 1½"
10½"
2½"
3½"
1½"

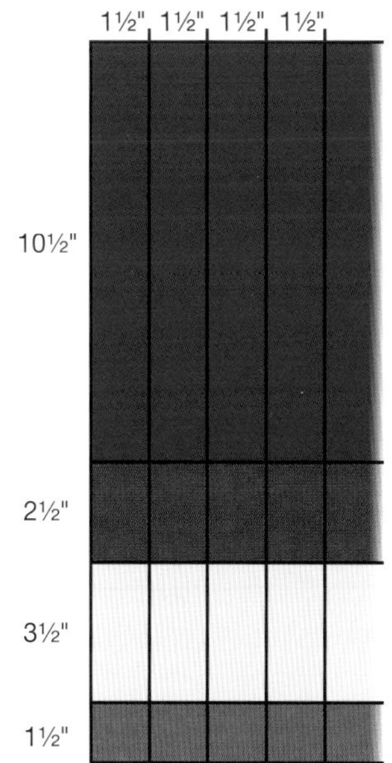

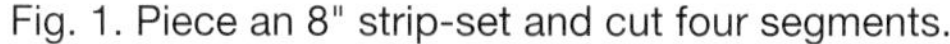

Fig. 1. Piece an 8" strip-set and cut four segments.

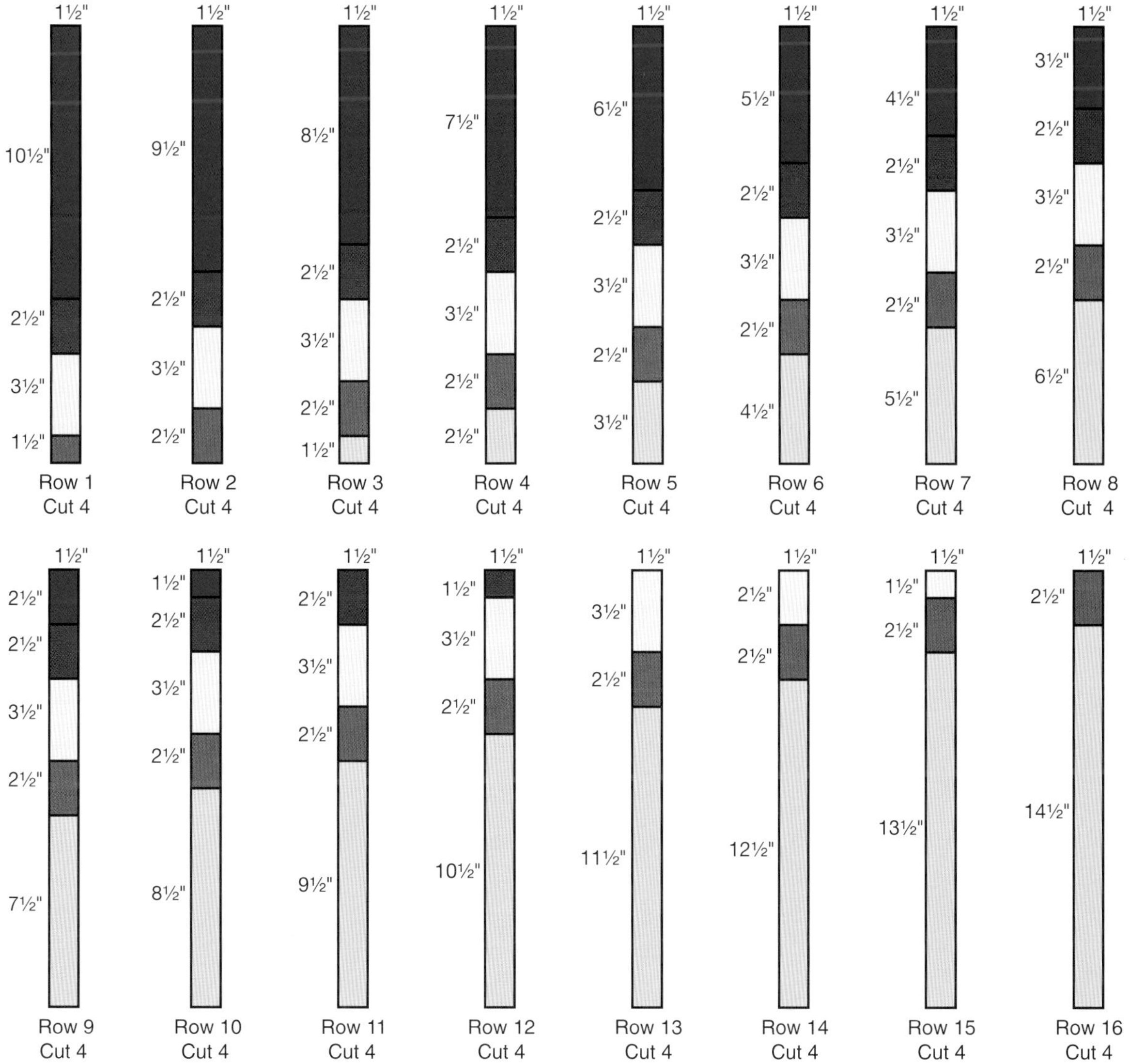

Row 1 Cut 4
Row 2 Cut 4
Row 3 Cut 4
Row 4 Cut 4
Row 5 Cut 4
Row 6 Cut 4
Row 7 Cut 4
Row 8 Cut 4
Row 9 Cut 4
Row 10 Cut 4
Row 11 Cut 4
Row 12 Cut 4
Row 13 Cut 4
Row 14 Cut 4
Row 15 Cut 4
Row 16 Cut 4

Fig. 2. Cut four segments for each row.

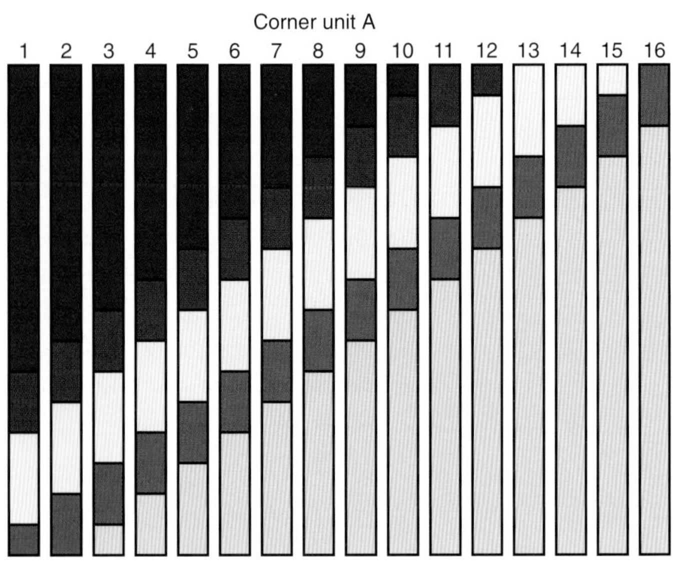

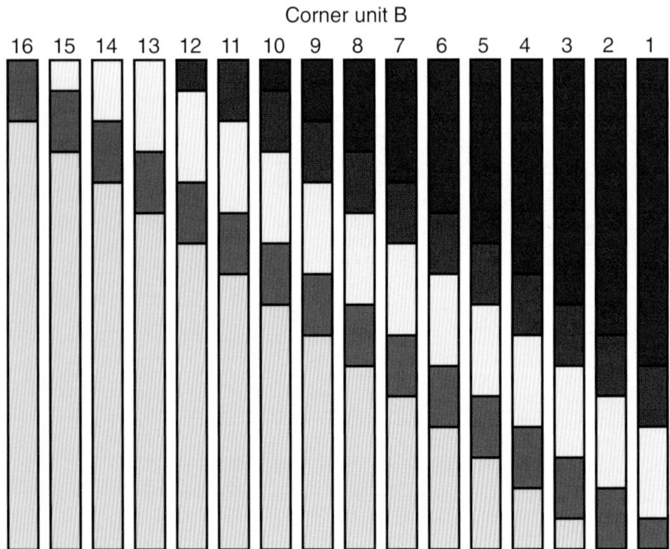

Fig. 3. Assemble two A units and two B units.

Making the Outer and Center Cross Units

1. For the outer cross blocks, piece the 42" gold and red strip-set shown in figure 4a. Press the seam allowances toward the dark fabric. Cut eight segments 4½" wide.

2. Piece the 8" gold and red strip-set shown in figure 4b. Press the seam allowance toward the dark fabric, and cut four segments 1½" wide.

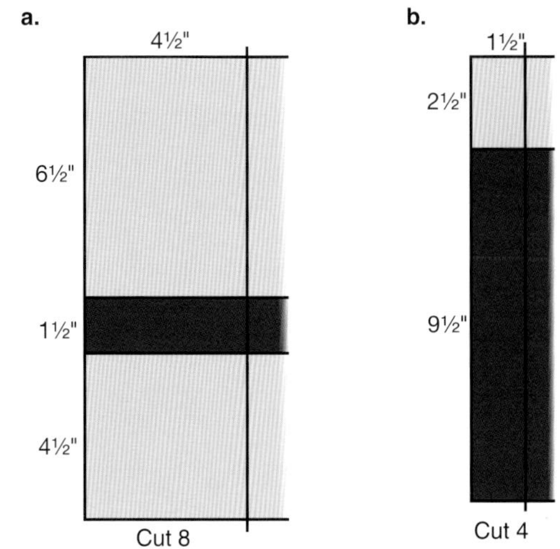

Fig. 4. Piece and cut segments for outer crosses.

3. Referring to the outer-cross diagram in figure 5, piece the gold and red strip-sets and the green and brown strips as shown. Press the seam allowances toward the darker fabric. Assemble four outer cross units.

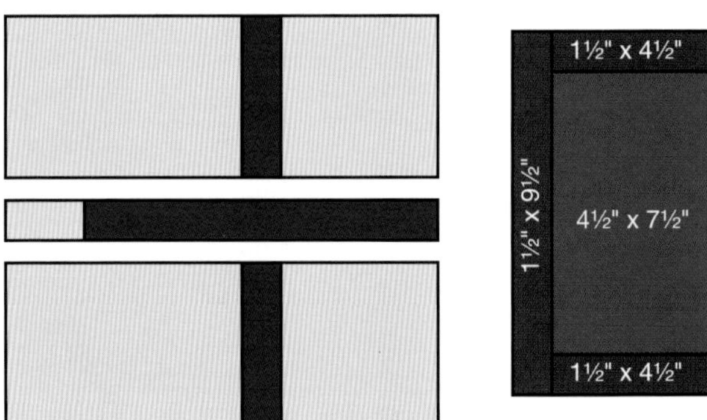

Fig. 5. Assemble four outer-cross units.

4. Piece an 8" brown and green strip-set (fig. 6). Press the seam allowance toward the darker fabric. Cut four segments 1½" wide.

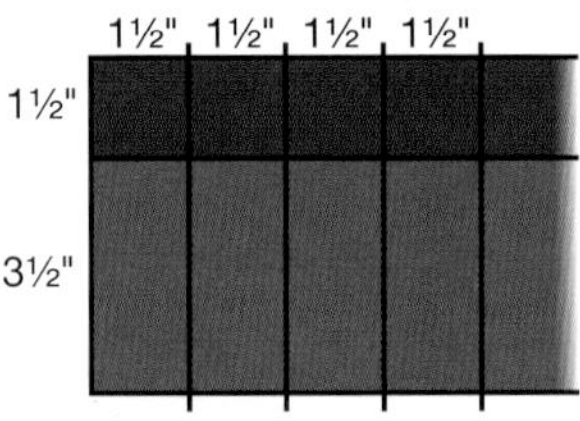

Fig. 6. Cut four segments for the center cross unit.

5. Using green and red pieces and the segments cut in step 4, make the center cross, as shown in figure 7.

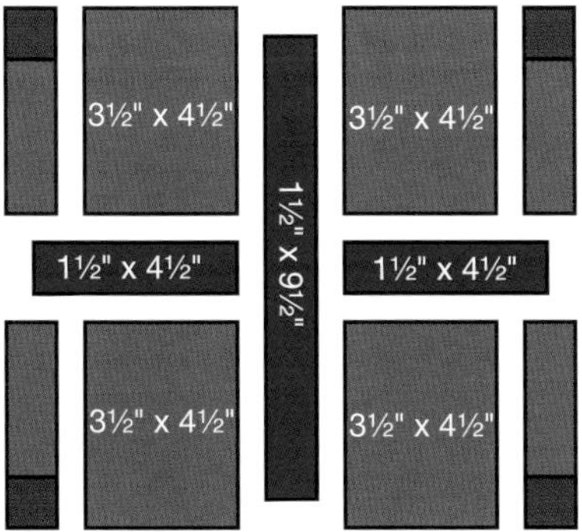

Fig. 7. Assemble the center cross unit.

Assembling and Finishing Your Quilt

1. Join your corner units, outer cross blocks, and the center cross according to the quilt assembly diagram in figure 8.

2. Using diagonal seams, sew the brown inner border strips together to form one long strip. Cut two strips 1½" x 41½". Sew these strips to the top and bottom edges of the quilt top. Press the seam allowances outward. Cut two strips 1½" x 43½". Sew these strips to each side of the quilt top, and press the seam allowances outward.

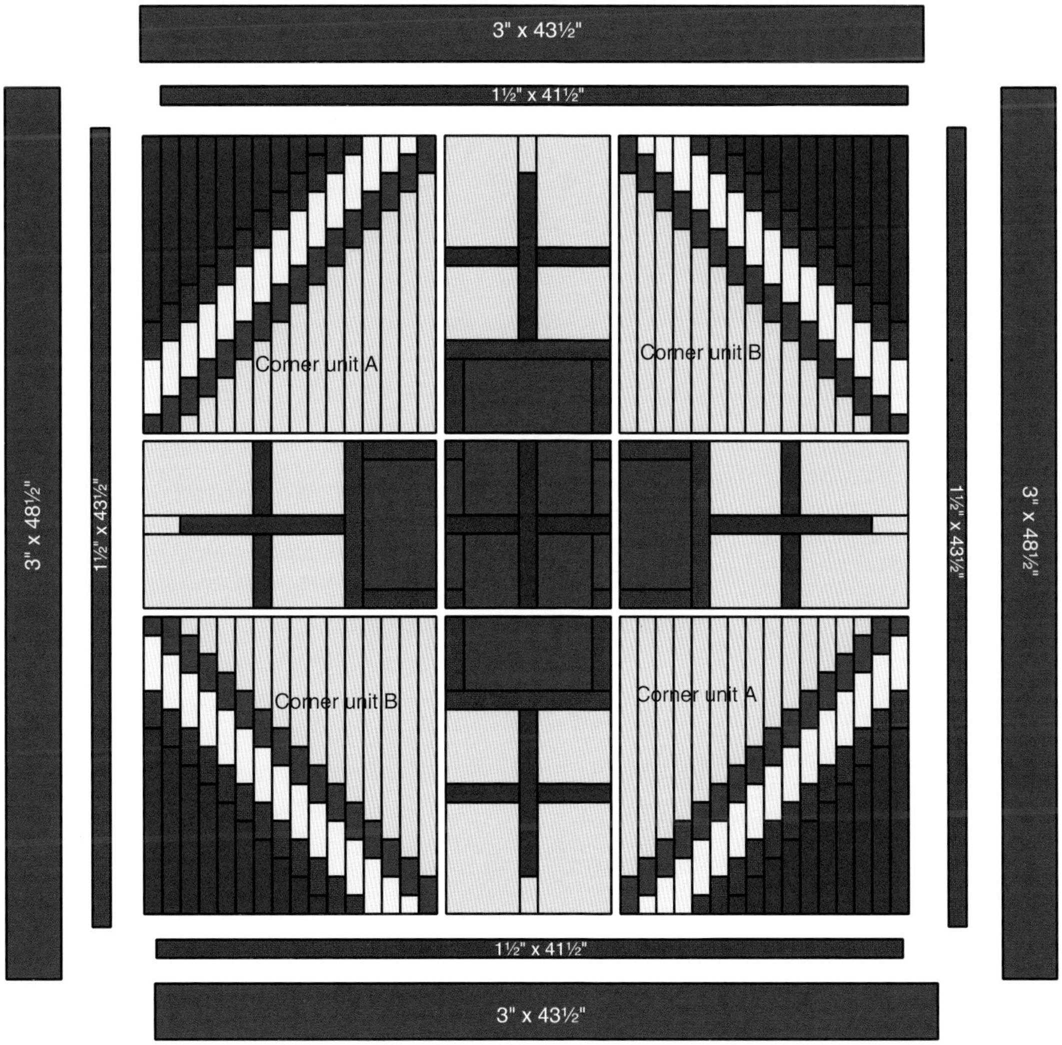

Fig. 8. Pueblo Cross quilt assembly

3. Using diagonal seams, sew the green outer border strips together to form one long strip. Cut two strips 3" x 43½". Sew these strips to the top and bottom edges of the quilt top. Press the seam allowances outward. Cut two strips 3" x 48½". Sew these strips to each side of the quilt top, and press seam allowances outward.

4. Layer the quilt top, batting, and backing. Baste the layers together. Quilt as desired. Bind the edges to finish.

PUEBLO CROSS II. Pieced by Jan Hightower, Roswell, New Mexico, and machine quilted by the author.

Finding Inspiration

When paired together, MIDNIGHT IN SANTA FE and PUEBLO CROSS II make a dramatic statement. The use of rich textural fabrics makes the pieces look like they are made of leather.

Rio Grande

RIO GRANDE table runner 14" x 50", four placemats 14" x 20". Made by the author.

Set a special table with this stunning table runner and placemat set. These are easy to piece and would make a great gift for anyone on your list. An antique Mexican weaving was the inspiration for this design. For a different look, try using four different shades of the same color with your background fabric.

Fabric requirements and cutting

Yardages are based on 42" wide fabric. All strips are cut across the width of the fabric.

Beige 1⅝ yd

Cut 1 strip 14½" x 42"
From this, cut
22 strips 14½" x 1½"
2 strips 14½" x 3"
Cut 2 strips 6½" x 42"
Cut 2 strips 4½" x 42"
Cut 2 strips 2½" x 42"
Cut 8 strips 1" x 42"

Blue 1 yd

Cut 5 strips 3" x 42"
From 1 strip, cut 2 strips 3" x 20"
Cut 1 strip 2½" x 42"
Cut 12 strips 1" x 42"

Brown ⅓ yd

Cut 8 strips 1" x 42"

Red 1 yd

Cut 1 strip 5½" x 42"
Cut 1 strip 3½" x 42"
From this, cut
2 strips 3½" x 20"
Cut 1 strip 1½" x 42"
Cut 12 strips 1" x 42"

Gold ⅝ yd

Cut 1 strip 3½" x 42"
From this, cut 1 strip 3½" x 20"
Cut 12 strips 1" x 42"

Batting 1 yd (96" wide)
See cutting layout on page 51.

Backing 2 yd See cutting layout on page 51.

Binding ⅞ yd (11 strips 2¼" x 42")

Piecing Your Rio Grande Table Runner and Placemats

1. Piece 12 gold, red, and blue strip-sets, as shown in figure 1. (See Tips on Strip Piecing on page 10.) Press the seam allowances in one direction. Cut the strip-sets into 24 segments for the X units.

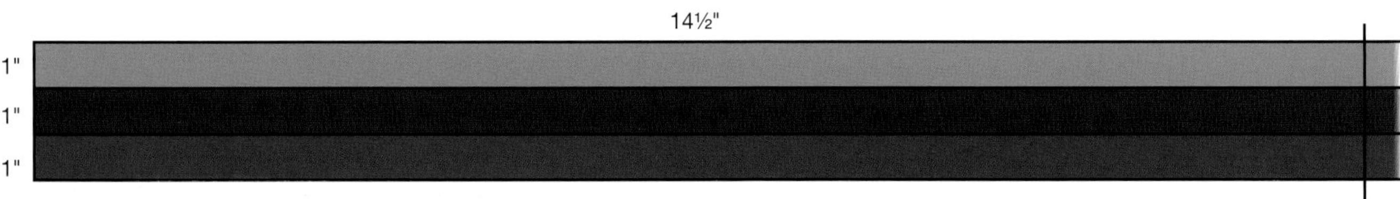

Fig. 1. Unit X. Cut 24 segments 14½" wide.

2. Piece four brown and beige strip-sets (fig. 2a). Press the seam allowances in one direction. Cut 84 segments 2" wide. Assemble 12 Y units, as shown in figure 2b.

3. To make the A units, piece the 20" blue, red, and gold strip-sets shown in figure 3. Press the seam allowances in one direction. Cut seven segments 1½" wide.

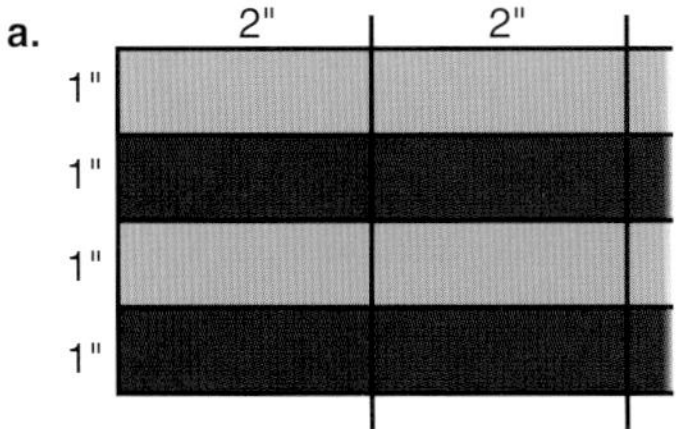

4. To make units B through D, piece one 42" strip-set each, as shown in figure 4. Cut 14 of each unit.

Finishing Your Rio Grande Table Runner and Placemats

1. Assemble one table runner and four placemats according to the assembly diagrams on page 50.

2. Referring to the cutting layout for the batting on page 51, cut the following pieces: For the table runner, cut one strip 18" x 54". For the placemats, cut four strips 16" x 22".

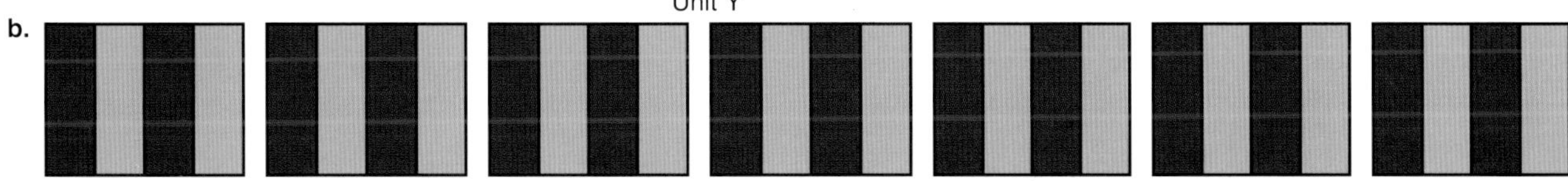

Fig. 2. Unit Y: (a.) Piece and cut 84 segments. (b.) Assemble 12 Y units.

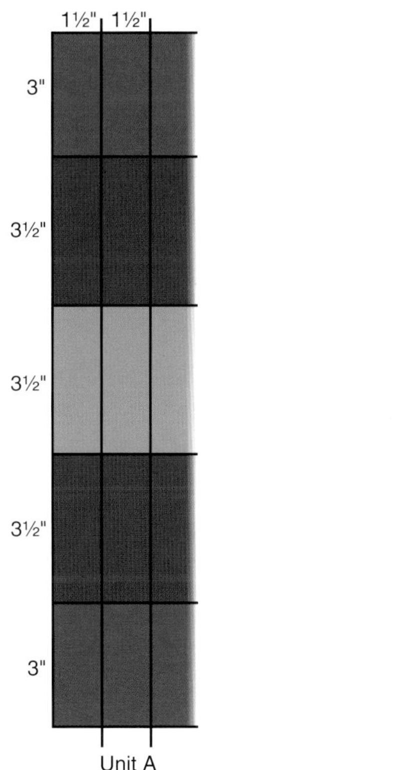

Fig. 3. A Units. Piece and cut seven segments.

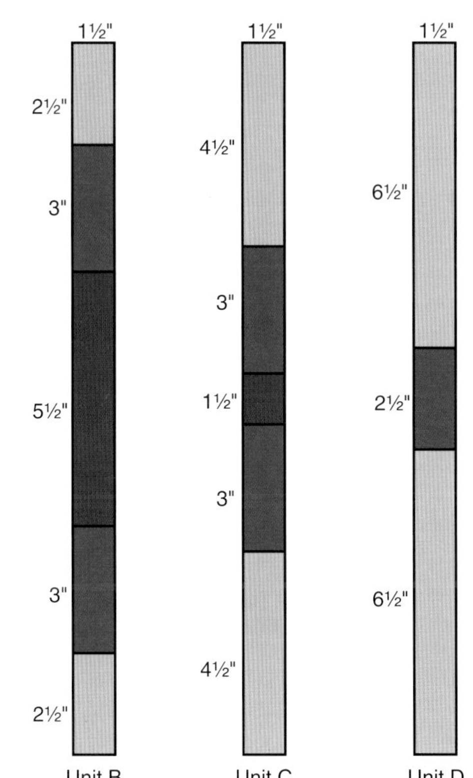

Fig. 4. Units B through D. Cut 14 of each.

3. Referring to the cutting layout for the backing on page 51, cut the following pieces: For the table runner, cut one strip 18" x 54". For the placemats, cut four strips 16" x 22".

4. To make units B throught D, piece one 42" strip set each as shown in figure 4. Cut 14 of each unit.

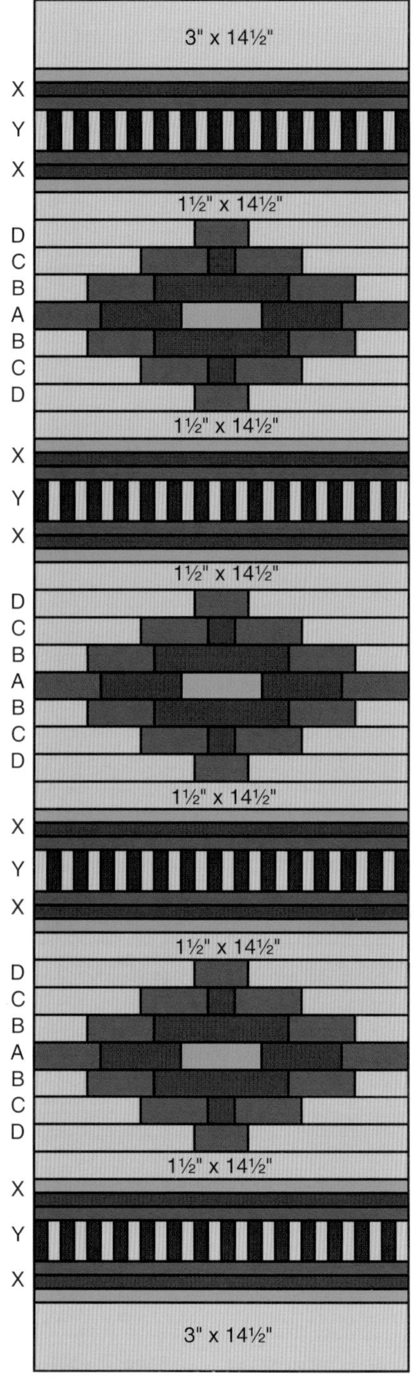

Table-runner assembly

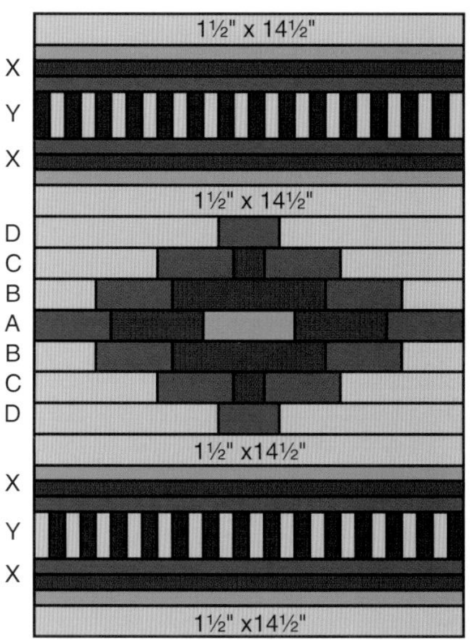

Placemat assembly

Fig. 5. Rio Grande placemat and table-runner assembly

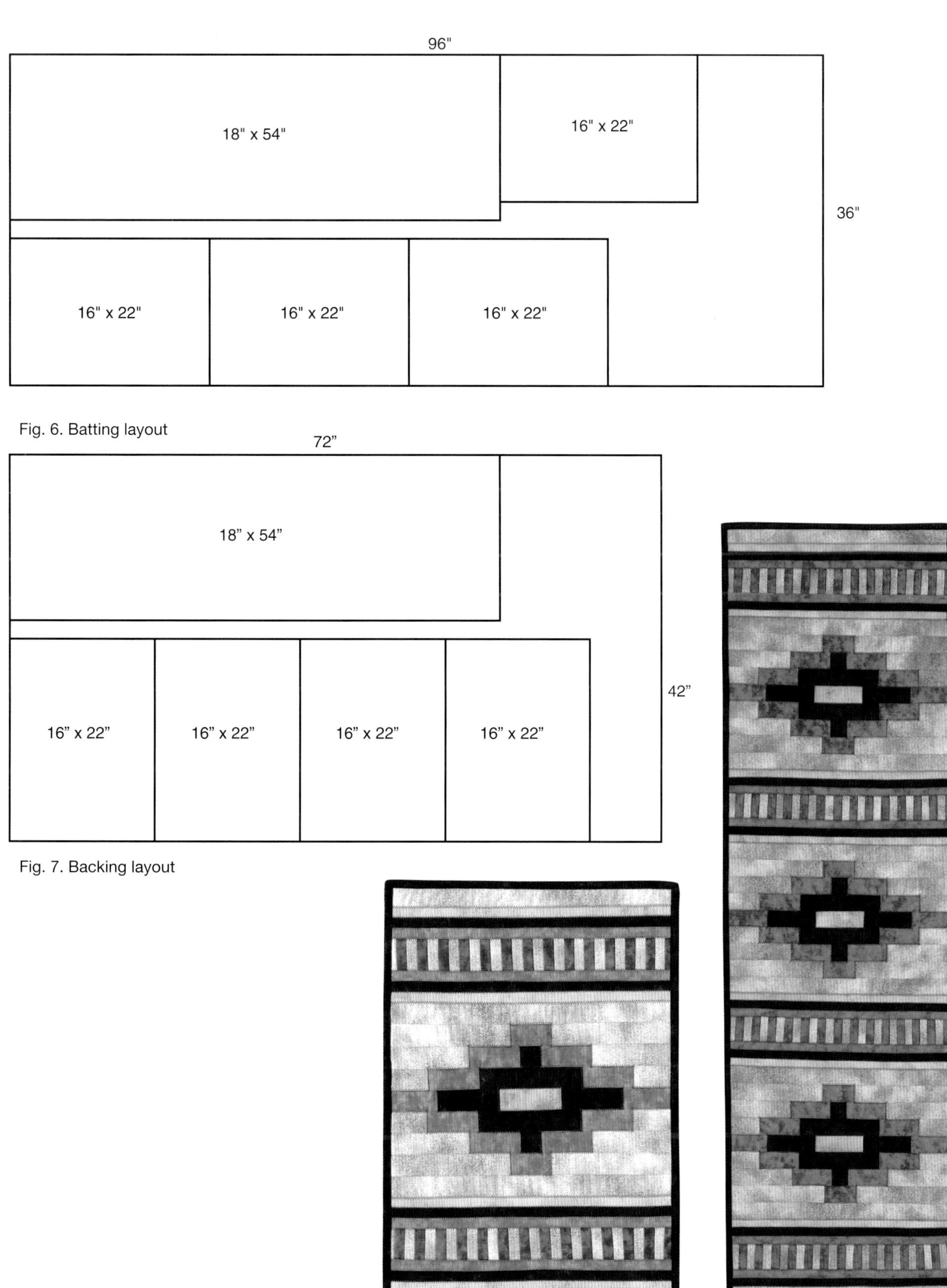

Fig. 6. Batting layout

Fig. 7. Backing layout

RIO GRANDE II. Made by Jan Hightower, Roswell, New Mexico.

Squash Blossom

Squash Blossom, 72" x 88". Pieced by the author. Quilted by Edith Stanton, Midland, Texas.

This quilt combines an easy block with a wide pieced sashing. When the blocks and pieced sashing are sewn together, a secondary design appears. Navajo Squash Blossom necklaces inspired my Squash Blossom block. This crescent-shaped pendant was introduced by the Spanish and is said to bring good luck. I recommend selecting a multicolored, medium-scale print for the main fabric and accenting it with other high-contrast fabrics for the best results.

Fabric requirements and cutting

Yardages are based on 42" wide fabric. All strips are cut across the width of the fabric.

Copper 1¼ yd

Pieced Blocks

Cut 4 strips 4½" x 42"

From these, cut

32 squares 4½" x 4½"

Inner Border

Cut 8 strips 2½" x 42"

Turquoise 2⅛ yd

Pieced Blocks

Cut 5 strips 4½" x 42"

From these, cut

80 strips 2½" x 4½"

Cut 18 strips 2½" x 42"

From these, cut

288 squares 2½" x 2½"

Purple Multicolor 2¾ yd

Pieced Blocks

Cut 7 strips 5½" x 42"

From these, cut

62 strips 4½" x 5½"

Cut 5 strips 2½" x 42"

From these, cut

80 squares 2½" x 2½"

Outer Border

Cut 9 strips 4½" x 42"

Batting 80" x 96"

Backing 5⅝ yd (2 lengths 95" pieced vertically)

Binding ¾ yd (9 strips 2½" x 42")

Cream 3¾ yd

Pieced Blocks

Cut 17 strips 4½" x 42"

From these, cut

80 squares 4½"

111 strips 2½" x 4½"

Cut 18 strips 2½" x 42"

From these, cut

284 squares 2½" x 2½"

Making the Squash Blossom Blocks and Pieced Sashing

1. Use 4½" cream and 2½" purple multicolor squares to make 80 corner-square A units, as shown in figure 1. (See Tips on Piecing Corner Square Units on page 9).

2. Use 2½" x 4½" cream and turquoise rectangles and the 2½" cream and turquoise squares to make 80 of each corner-square units B and C (fig. 2). Then join them to make 80 BC units.

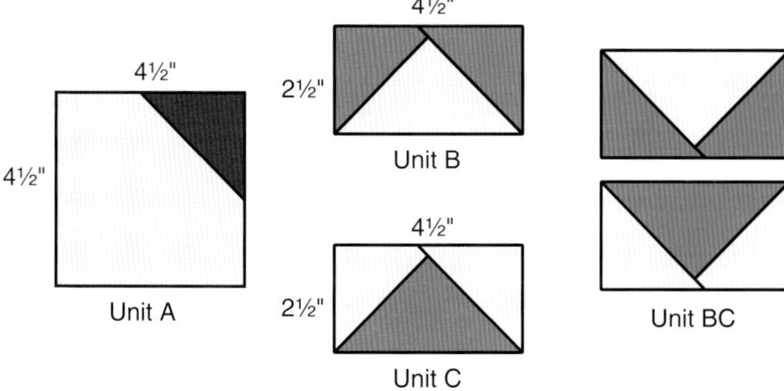

Fig. 1. Unit A. Make 80. Fig. 2. Unit BC. Make 80 of each.

3. Piece 32 D units from the 4½" copper squares and the 2½" turquoise squares (fig. 3).

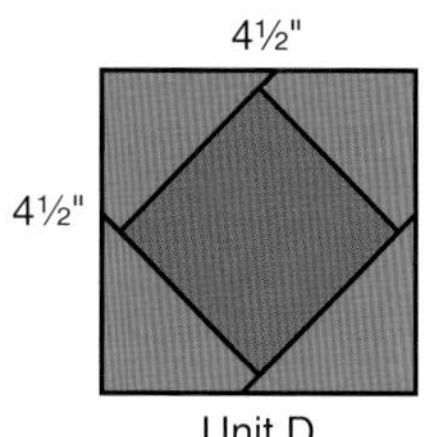

Fig. 3. Unit D. Make 32.

4. Join units from steps 1 through 3 as shown in figure 4, then assemble 20 blocks (fig. 4).

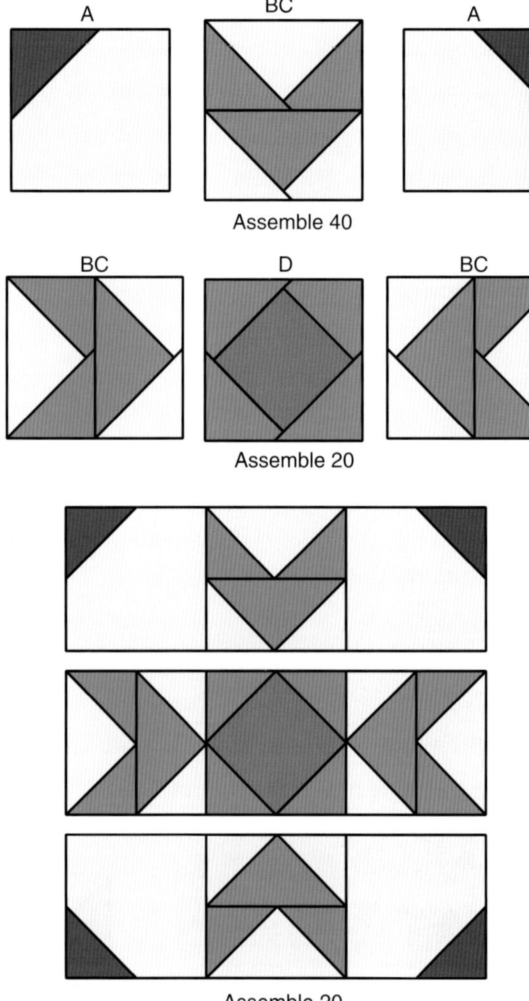

Fig. 4. SQUASH BLOSSOM block assembly

5. Use the 2½" cream squares and 4½" x 5½" purple multicolor rectangles to make 62 E units, as shown in figure 5. Then assemble 31 sashing F units.

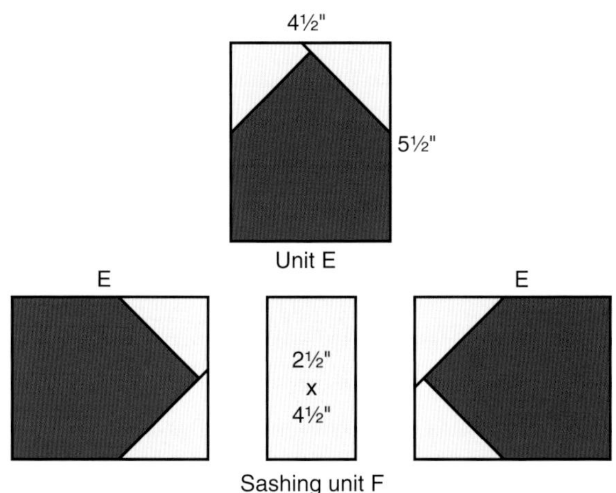

Fig. 5. Make 62 E units. Assemble 31 sashing F units.

6. Assemble five block rows and four sashing rows (fig. 6).

Assembling and Finishing Your Quilt

1. Sew your block and sashing rows according to the quilt diagram on page 56. Press the seam allowances toward the F units. Join the rows, and press the seam allowances in one direction.

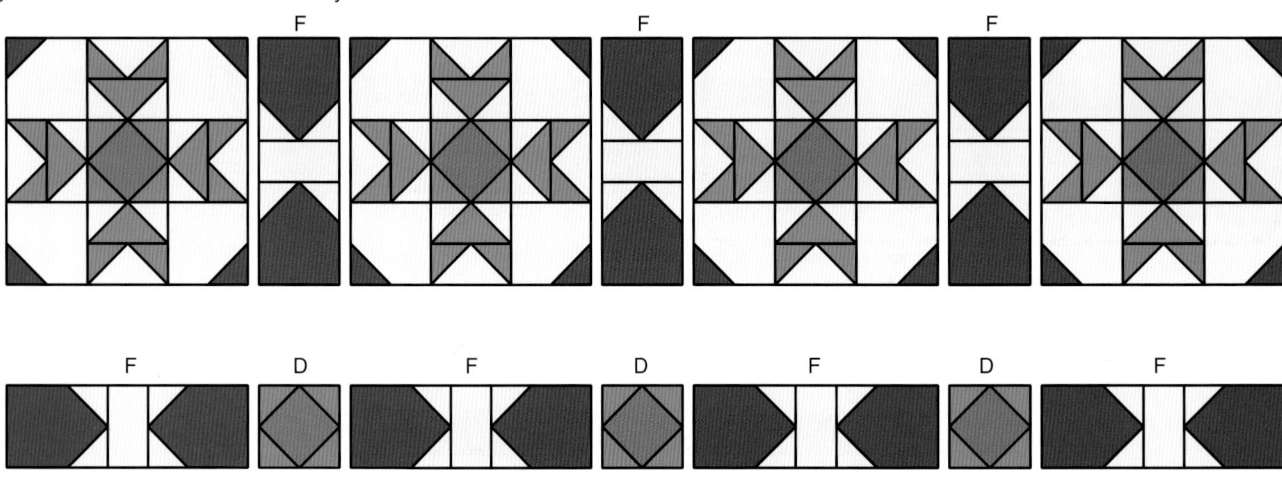

Fig. 6. Block and sashing rows

2. Using diagonal seams, sew the eight copper inner border strips together to form one long strip. Cut two strips 2½" x 60½". Sew these strips to the top and bottom edges of the quilt top. Press the seam allowances outward. Cut two strips 2½" x 80½". Sew these strips to each side of the quilt top, and press seam allowances outward.

3. Using diagonal seams, sew the nine purple multicolor outer border strips together to form one long strip. Cut two strips 4½" x 64½". Sew these strips to the top and bottom edges of the quilt top. Press the seam allowances outward. Cut two strips 4½" x 88½". Sew these strips to each side of the quilt top, and press seam allowances outward.

4. Layer the quilt top, batting, and backing. Baste the layers together. Quilt as desired. Bind the edges to finish.

Fig. 7. Squash Blossom quilt assembly

Squash Blossom

Wallhanging

Squash Blossom Black, 34" x 34". Pieced by Marion Wessel, Roswell, New Mexico.

Fabric requirements and cutting

Yardages are based on 42" wide fabric. All strips are cut across the width of the fabric.

Turquoise Multicolor ¾ yd

Pieced Blocks

Cut 1 strip 5½" x 42"
From this, cut 8 strips 4½" x 5½"
Cut 1 strip 2½" x 42"
From this, cut 16 strips 2½" x 2½"

Outer Border

Cut 4 strips 2½" x 42"
From these, cut
2 strips 2½" x 30½"
2 strips 2½" x 34½"

Turquoise ⅝ yd

Pieced Blocks

Cut 1 strip 4½" x 42"
From this, cut
16 strips 2½" x 4½"
Cut 4 strips 2½" x 42"
From these, cut
52 squares 2½" x 2½"

Lime Green ½ yd

Pieced Blocks

Cut 1 strip 4½" x 42"
From this, cut 5 squares 4½" x 4½"

Inner Border

Cut 4 strips 1½" x 42"
From these, cut
2 strips 1½" x 28"
2 strips 1½" x 30½"

Black ⅞ yd

Pieced Blocks

Cut 3 strips 4½" x 42"
From these, cut
16 squares 4½" x 4½"
20 strips 2½" x 4½"
Cut 3 strips 2½" x 42"
From these, cut
48 squares 2½" x 2½"

Batting 40" x 40"

Backing 1⅛ yd (40" x 40")

Binding ⅓ yd (4 strips 2½" x 42")

Making a Squash Blossom Wallhanging

The piecing and assembly instructions for the SQUASH BLOSSOM wallhanging pictured on page 56 are the same as the instructions for the quilt. The number of units to piece and assemble are shown in figures 8 through 11.

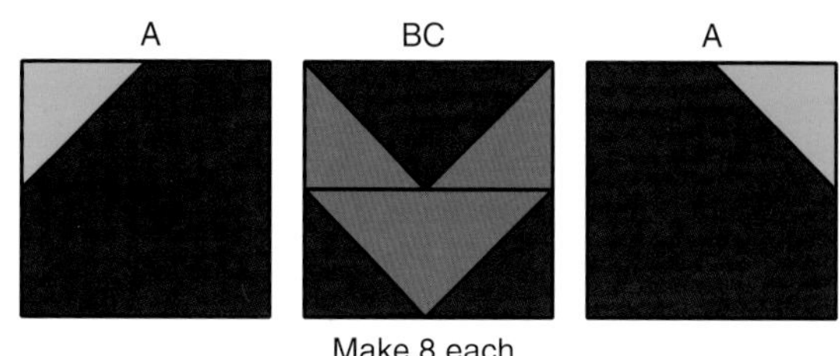

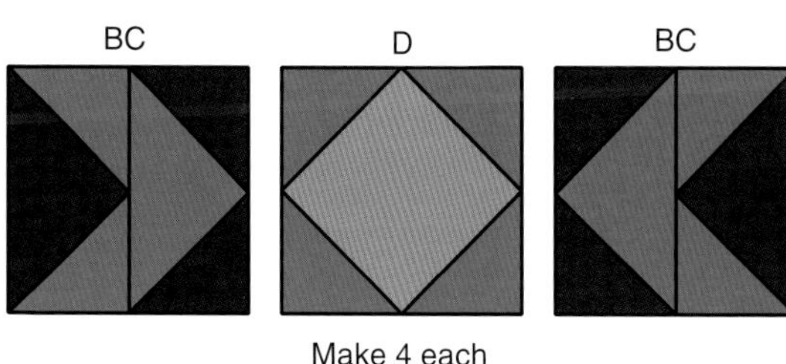

Fig. 8. Piece units A, BC, and D.

Fig. 9. Block assembly

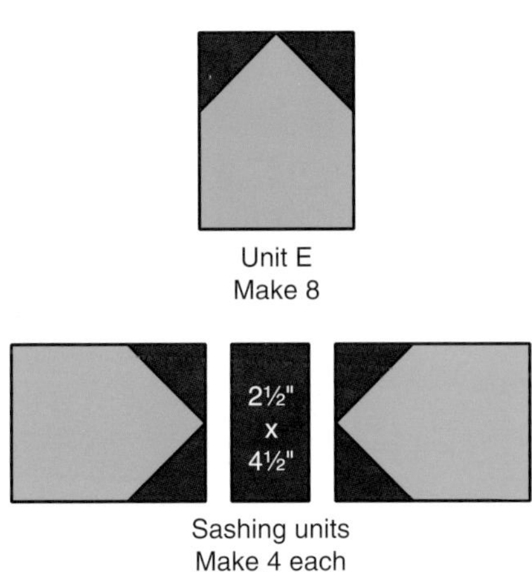

Fig. 10. Piece eight E units and assemble four sashing units.

Fig. 11 SQUASH BLOSSOM wallhanging assembly

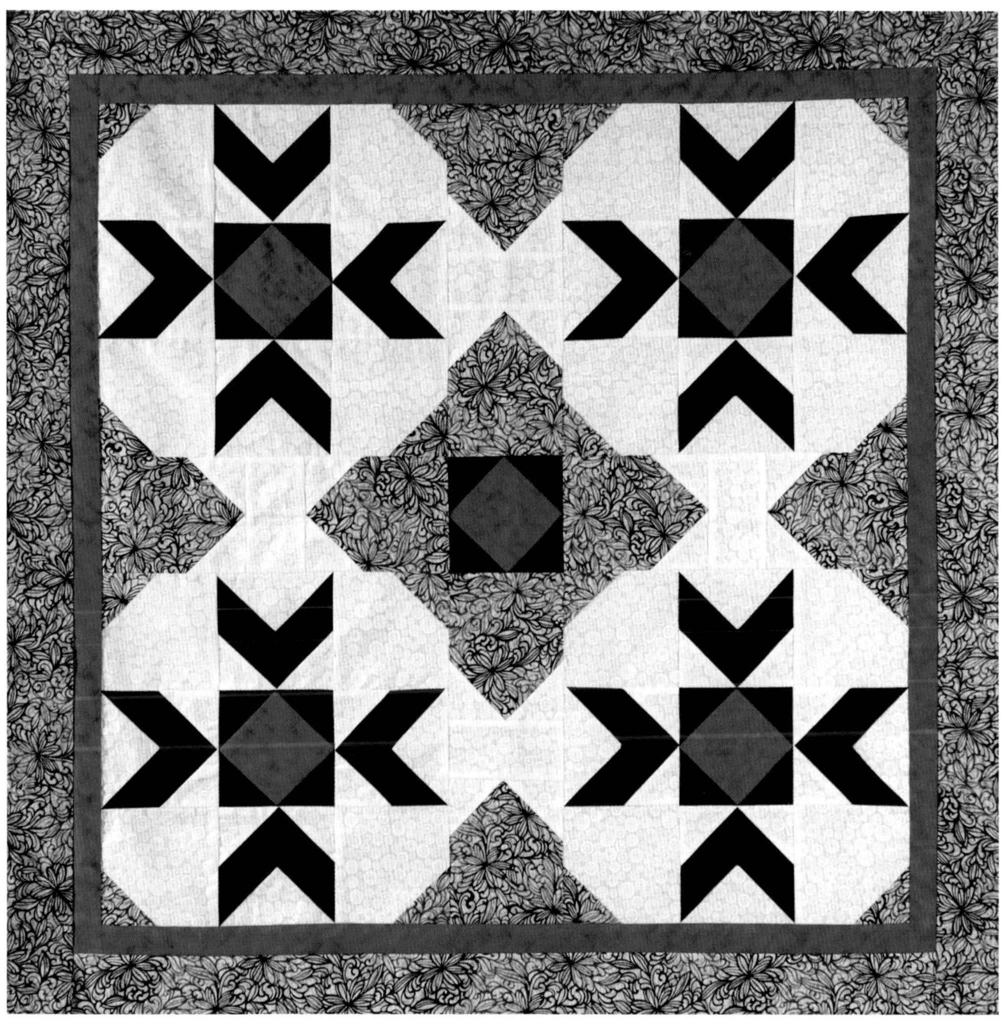

Squash Blossom White, 34" x 34". Pieced by Marion Wessel, Roswell, New Mexico.

Finding Inspiration

There are as many varieties of Squash Blossom necklaces as there are artists that create them. The shape of the bead is said to resemble a squash blossom. Some of these necklaces are made entirely of silver, while others are accented with turquoise. Squash Blossom necklaces have a large open crescent-shaped pendant, called a *naja* (meaning "crescent" in Navajo). I find inspiration for my quilts in both the colors and the shapes in these necklaces from the Southwest.

Turquoise Beauty

TURQUOISE BEAUTY, 46" x 61½". Pieced by the author. Quilted by Richard Larson, Plano, Texas.

My inspiration for this quilt was the beautiful inlay and channelwork jewelry that is so popular in the Southwest. Jewelry artists create intricate patchwork pieces using natural stone and metal. Inlay jewelry is created when the artist places each stone or shell touching each other. Channelwork jewelry is a type of inlay where a sliver of silver surrounds each stone or shell. The turquoise stone is known as "the sky stone." Its color can range from the palest of green to a deep blue. The Mexicans taught the Navajo how to work with silver. Then it spread to other pueblos. When travelers started coming to New Mexico in the 1890s, the demand for turquoise jewelry boomed. Turquoise jewelry, whether old or new, is still very collectible today.

Fabric requirements and cutting

Yardages are based on 42" wide fabric. All strips are cut across the width of the fabric.

Turquoise 2½ yd

Cut 1 strip 5" x 42"
Cut 3 strips 4½" x 42"
Cut 4 strips 3½" x 42"
Cut 16 strips 3" x 42"

Black 1⅛ yd

Cut 33 strips 1" x 42"
From 14 strips, cut
20 strips 1" x 15½" (strips I)
24 strips 1" x 9½" (strips J)

Batting 54" x 70"
Backing 3 yd (2 lengths 52", pieced horizontally)
Binding ½ yd (6 strips 2½" x 42")

Making Turquoise Beauty Block Units

1. Piece six turquoise and black strip-sets, as shown in figure 1. Press the seam allowances away from the narrow strips.

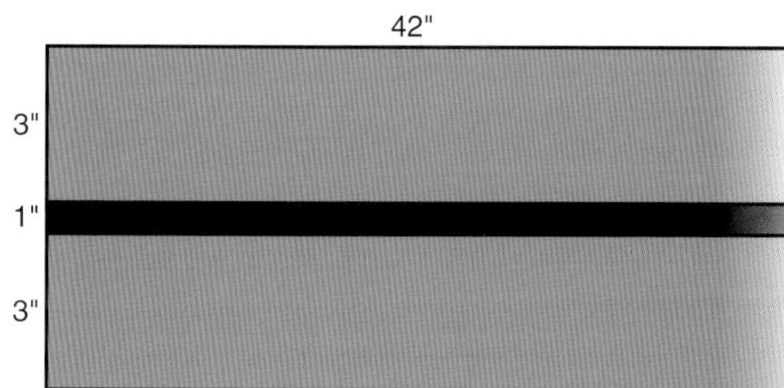

Fig. 1. Piece six strip-sets.

2. Cut the strip-sets into segments A, B, and C, as shown in figure 2.

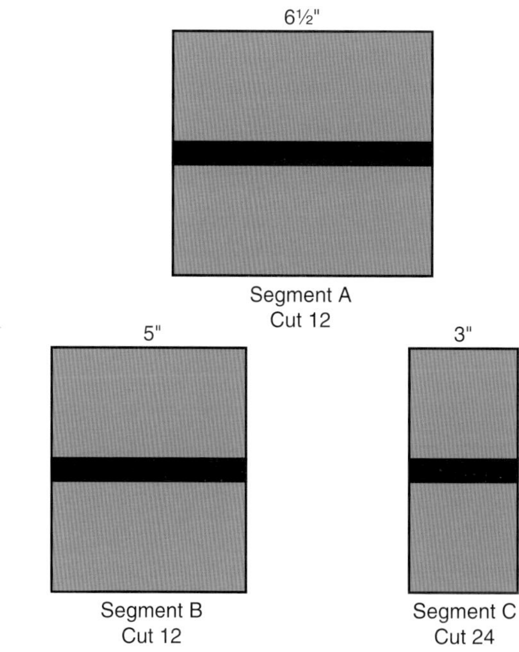

Fig. 2. Cut segments A, B, and C.

3. For segments D through H, piece turquoise and black strip-sets, as shown in figure 3. Press the seam allowances away from the narrow strips. Cut segments as shown.

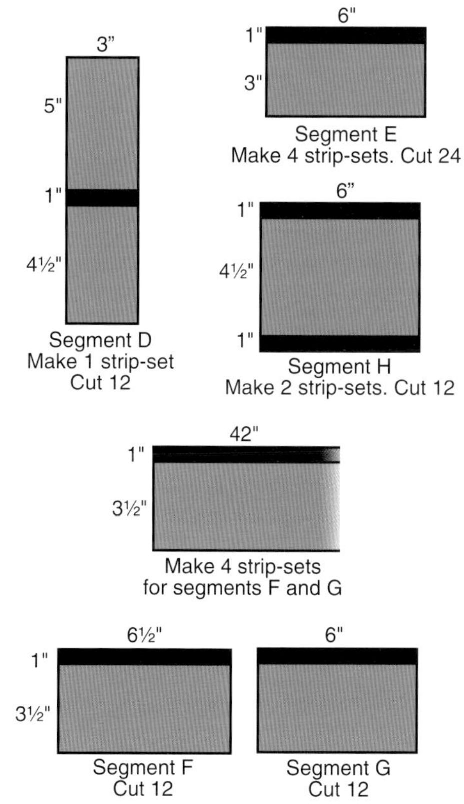

Fig. 3. Segments D through H

4. Assemble 12 V units, using J strips and segments A and E, as shown in figure 4. Press the seam allowances away from the narrow strips.

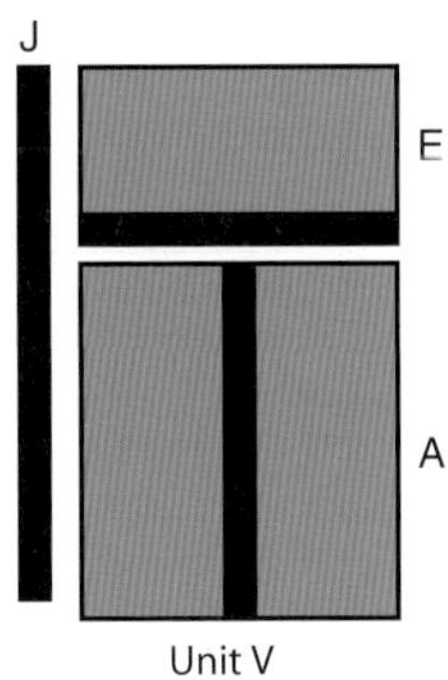

Fig. 4. Assemble 12 V units.

5. Assemble 12 W units, using units C, F, and G (fig. 5). Press the seam allowances away from the narrow strips.

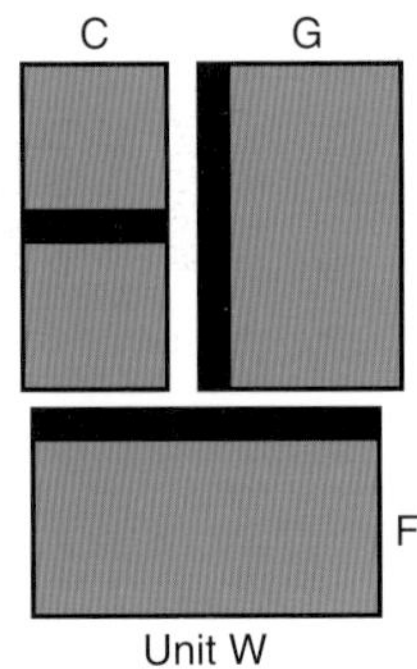

Fig. 5. Assemble 12 units W.

6. Assemble 12 X units, using J strips and D segments, as shown in figure 6. Press the seam allowances away from the narrow strips.

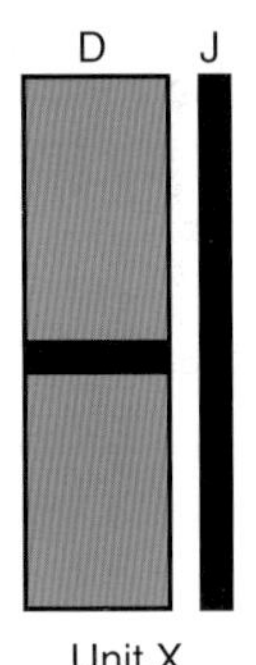

Fig. 6. Assemble 12 X units.

7. Assemble 12 Y units, using segments C and E, as shown in figure 7. Press the seam allowances away from the narrow strips.

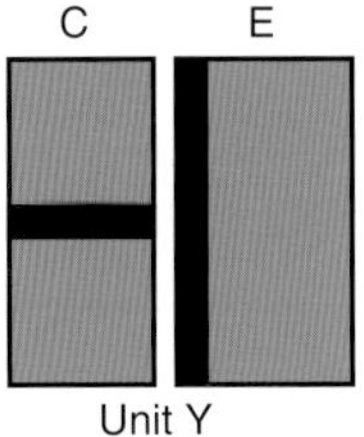

Fig. 7. Assemble 12 Y units.

8. Assemble 12 Z units, using segments B and H, as shown in figure 8. Press the seam allowances away from the narrow strips.

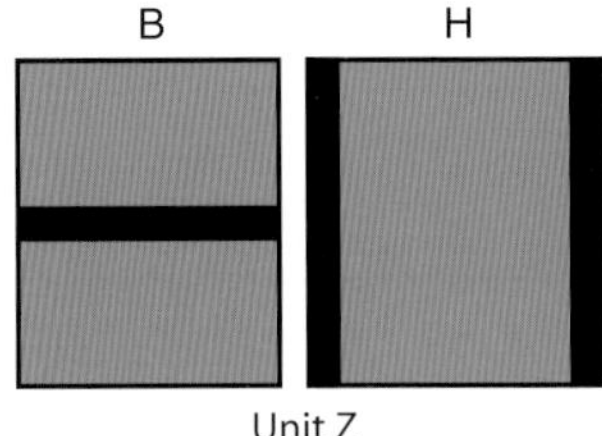

Fig. 8. Assemble 12 Z units.

Making Turquoise Beauty Blocks

1. Assemble 12 S block sections, using I strips and units V, W, and X, as shown in figure 9. Press the seam allowances away from the narrow strips.

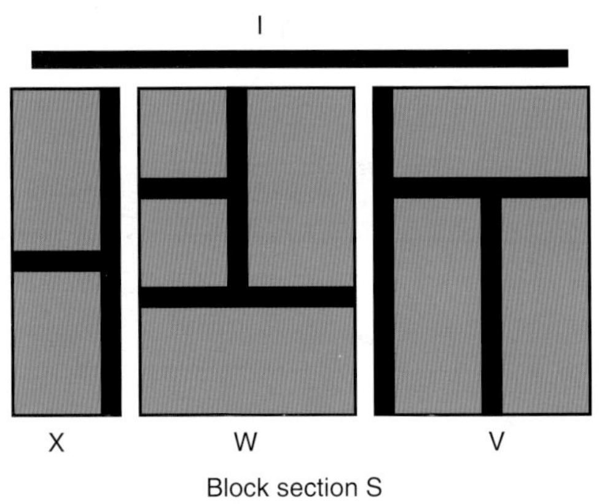

Fig. 9. Assemble 12 S block sections.

2. Assemble 12 T block sections, using units Y and Z, as shown in figure 10. Press the seam allowances away from the narrow strips.

3. Assemble 12 blocks, using sections S and T, according to the block assembly diagram in figure 11. Press the seam allowances away from the narrow strips.

Z Y

Block section T

Fig. 10. Assemble 12 T block sections.

Assembling and Finishing Your Quilt

1. Assemble four rows, referring to the row assembly diagram in figure 12. Press the seam allowances away from the narrow strips. *Notice that the center block in each row is rotated clockwise one turn.*

2. Using diagonal seams, sew four black 1" x 42" strips to form one long strip. Cut three strips 1" x 46½".

3. Join the rows according to the quilt assembly diagram on page 64. Press the seam allowances in one direction.

4. Layer the quilt top, batting, and backing. Baste the layers together. Quilt as desired. Bind the edges to finish.

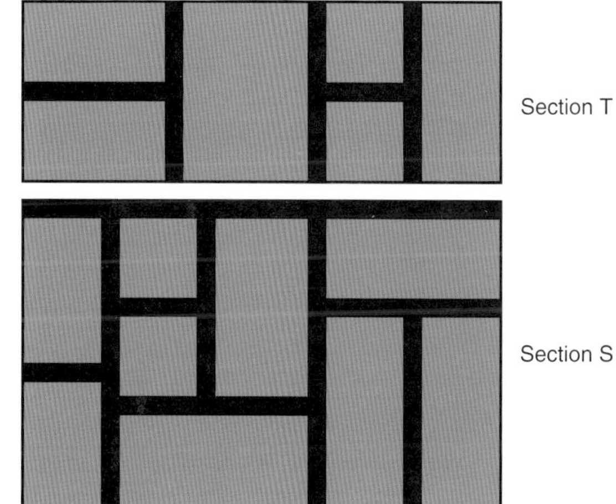

Fig. 11. Turquoise Beauty block assembly

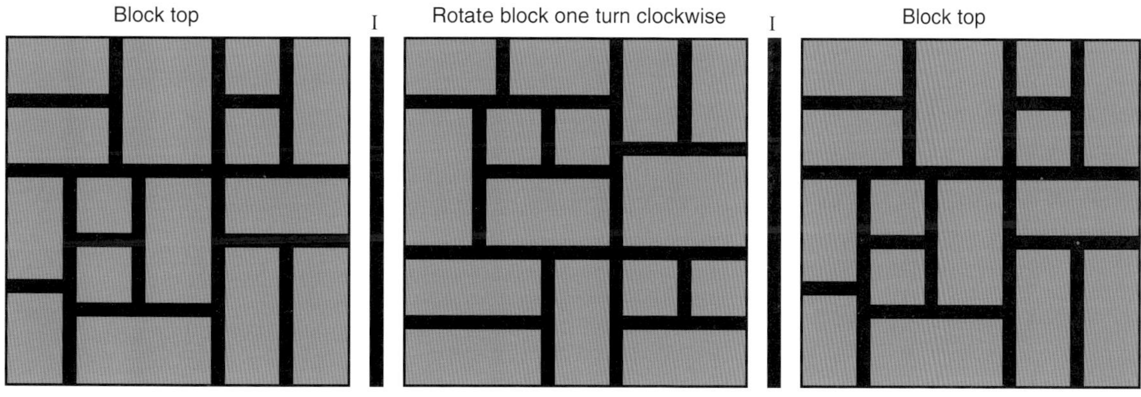

Fig. 12. Row assembly

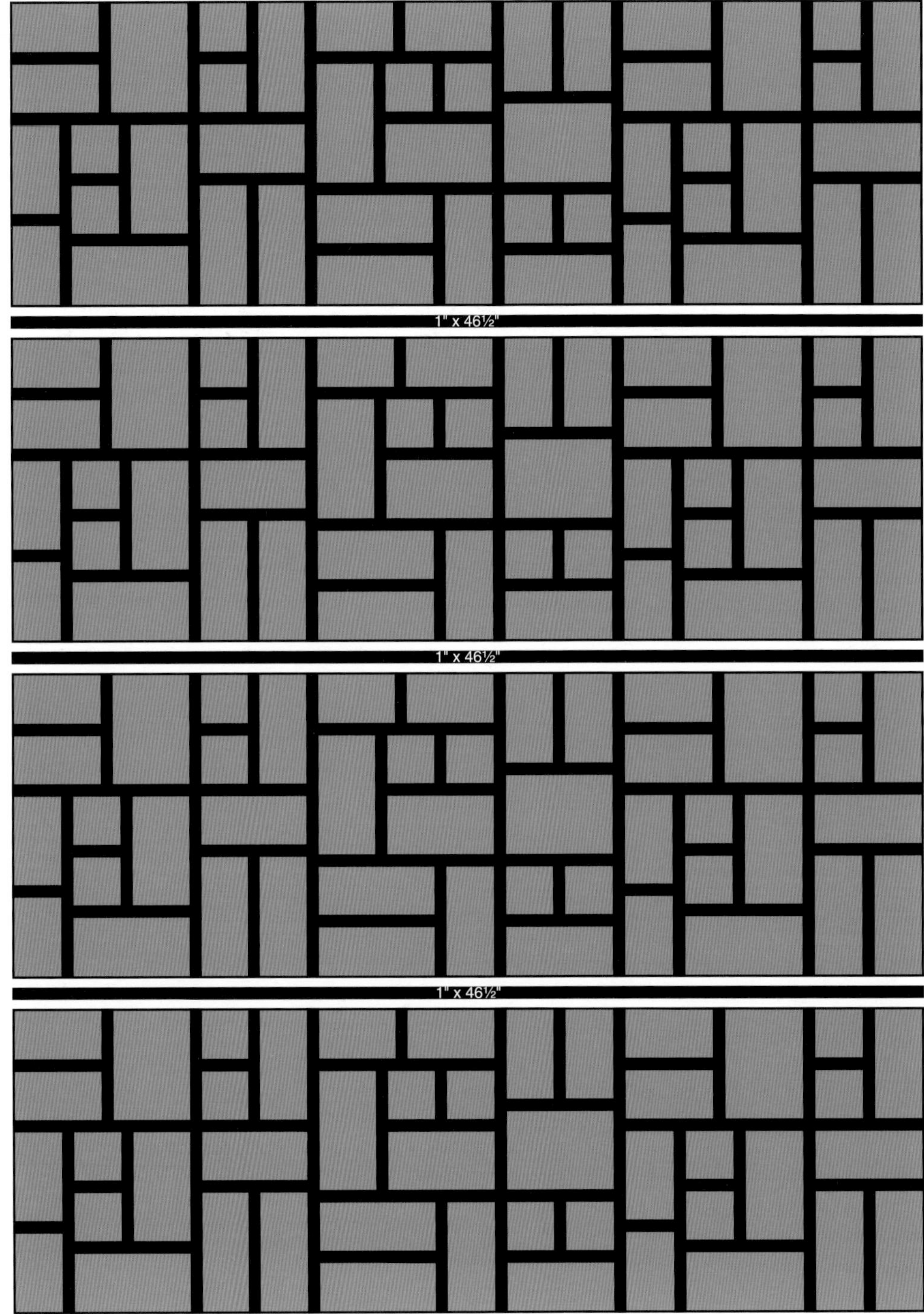

Fig. 13. Turquoise Beauty quilt assembly

Stones of a Different Color

STONES OF A DIFFERENT COLOR. 30½" x 30½". Made by the author.

The different stone-colored fabrics I chose for this quilt mimic the rich colors of southwestern gemstones—blue lapis, yellow-green peridot, red coral, orange spiny oyster, purple sugilite, and of course, turquoise.

Fabric requirements and cutting

Yardages are based on 42" wide fabric. All strips are cut across the width of the fabric.

Turquoise ⅓ yd

Cut 2 strips 3" x 42"

Gray ¾ yd

Cut 16 strips 1" x 42"
From these, cut 6 strips into
1 strip 1" x 31"
6 strips 1" x 15½"
8 strips 1" x 9½"

Purple ½ yd

Cut 2 strips 4½" x 42"
Cut 1 strip 3" x 42"

Red ½ yd

Cut 1 strip 3½" x 42"
Cut 2 strips 3" x 42"

Orange ⅓ yd

Cut 1 strip 5" x 42"
Cut 1 strip 3" x 42"

Yellow Green ⅓ yd

Cut 1 strip 3½" x 42"
Cut 1 strip 3" x 42"

Blue ⅛ yd

Cut 1 strip 3" x 42"

Batting 36" x 36"
Backing 1 yd (36" x 36")
Binding ⅓ yd (4 strips 2½" x 42")

Making Stones of a Different Color Units

1. Piece 2 strip-sets, as shown in figure 14. Press the seam allowances away from the narrow strip. Cut strip-sets into segments A and B, as shown.

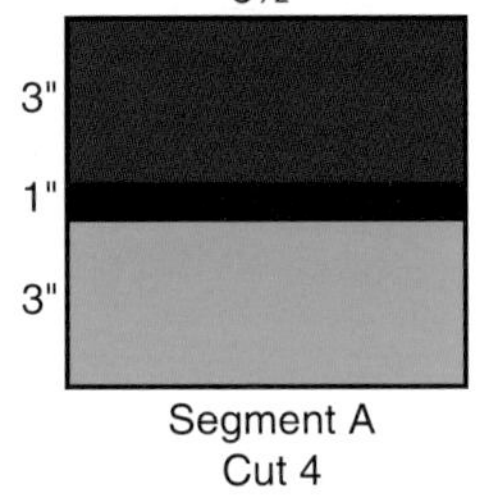

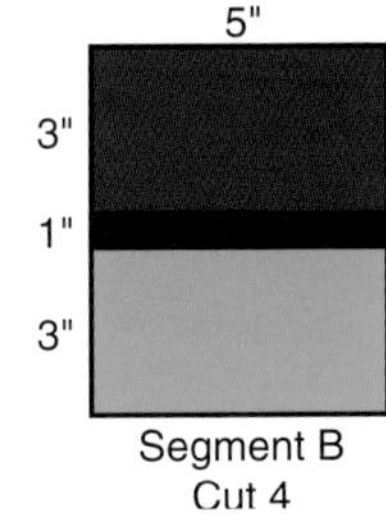

Fig. 14. Cut segments A and B.

2. Piece strip-sets and cut segments C through I, as shown in figure 15.

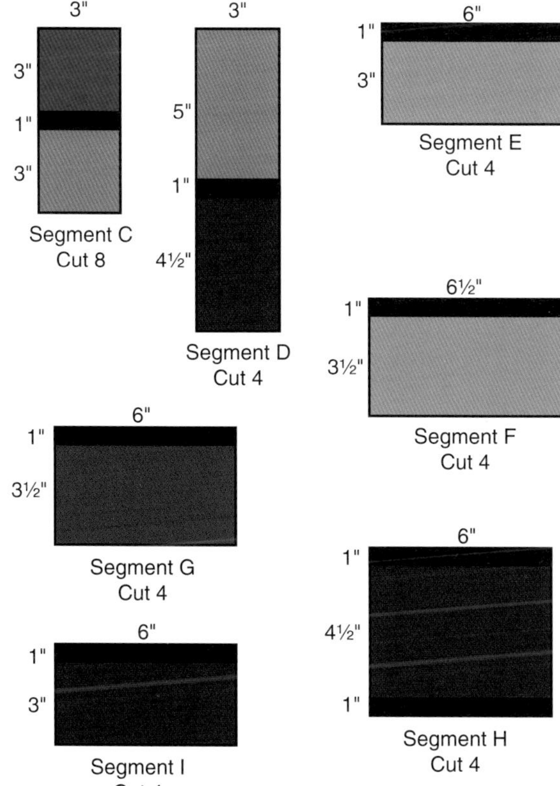

Fig. 15. Segments C through I

3. Sew four V units and four W units (fig. 16). Press the seam allowances away from the narrow strips.

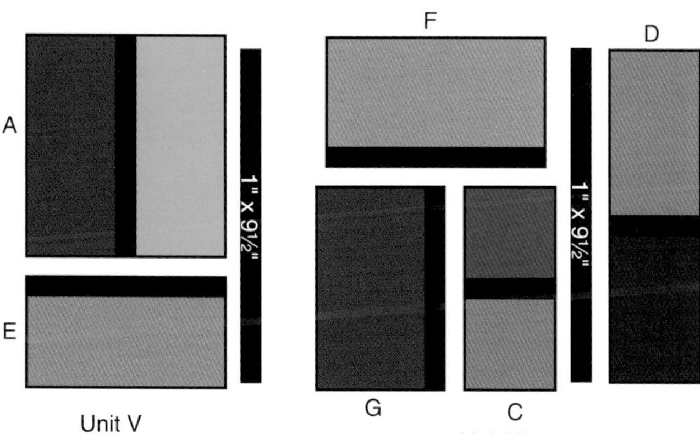

Fig. 16. Units V and W

4. Assemble four X block sections and four Y sections, as shown in figure 17.

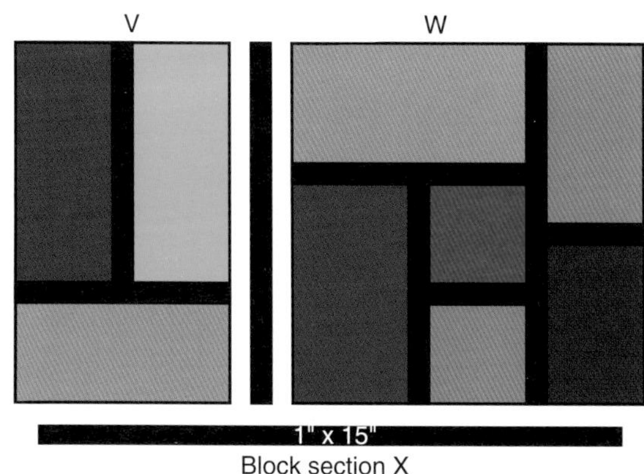

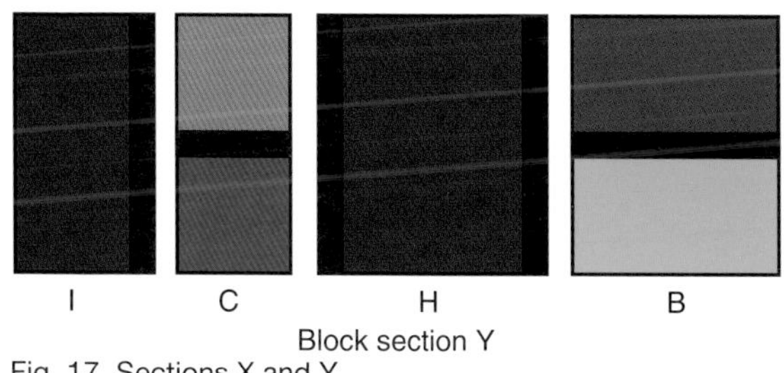

Fig. 17. Sections X and Y

5. Assemble 4 blocks (fig. 18).

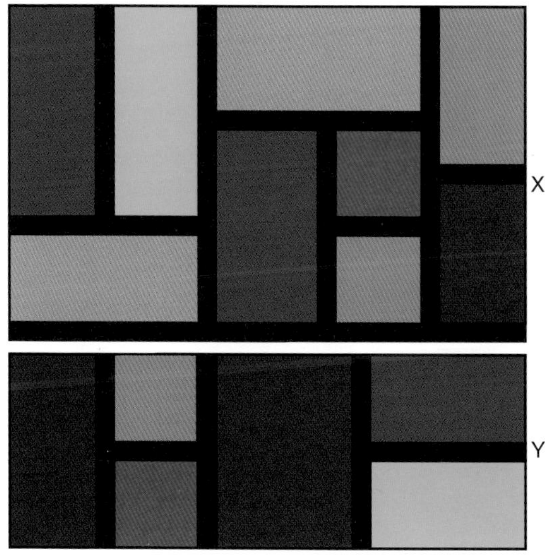

Fig. 18. Block assembly

6. Sew blocks together according to the quilt assembly diagram.

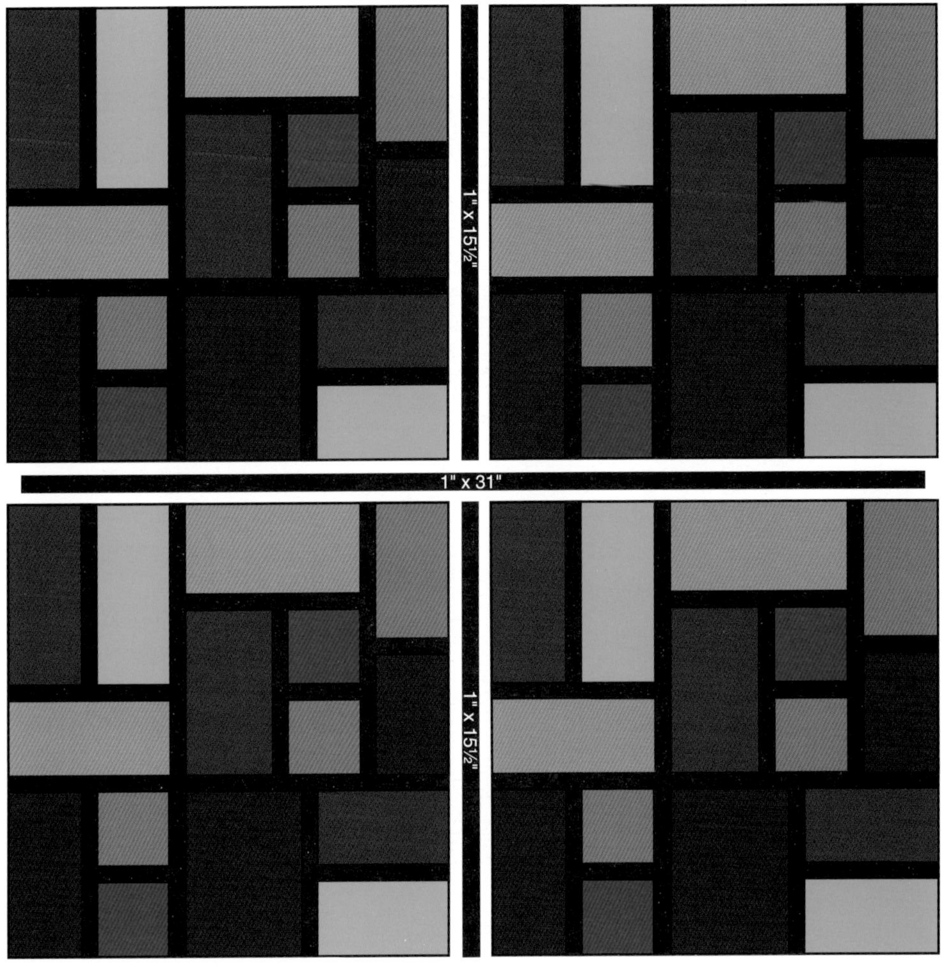

Fig. 19. STONES OF A DIFFERENT COLOR quilt assembly

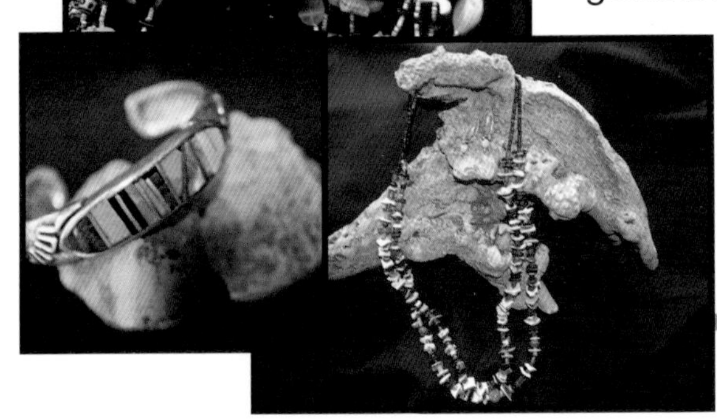

Finding Inspiration

These pieces show the variety of different colors in the gemstones used in southwestern jewelry. The small slivers of colored stones set in silver on the cuff bracelet inspired the STONES OF A DIFFERENT COLOR wallhanging. Most multi-strand necklaces of the Southwest define the center of each strand with a graduation of beads, using the heavier beads to add weight to the center.

Ancient Acoma

ANCIENT ACOMA 48" x 48". Made by the author. Quilted by Edith Stanton, Midland, Texas. Block size: 12" x 12".

The Acoma Indians are fine weavers and basket makers, but are best known for their striking pottery. Ancient Acoma pottery shards were the inspiration for this contemporary wall quilt. Raw clay is taken from the earth and shaped by the hands of a potter. Hand-shaped pots are fired and hand painted for everyday and ceremonial use. Acoma potters are known for complex interlocking designs that cover most of the vessel. The complex design units were filled with red, yellow, and orange slip, black paint, and fine-lined hatch strokes.

Although the instructions given are for machine appliqué, remember that hand appliqué is also an option. Seam allowances need to be added to each appliqué piece if you choose to hand appliqué.

Fabric requirements and cutting

Yardages are based on 42" wide fabric. All strips are cut across the width of the fabric.

Background 2¼ yd

Cut 6 strips 12½" x 42"
From these, cut 16 squares 12½" x 12½"

Rust 2 yd

Appliqué Pieces
16 pieces from template B
16 pieces from template D

Black 2 yd

Appliqué Pieces
16 pieces from template A
16 pieces from template C

Batting 54" x 54"
Backing 3¼ yd (2 lengths 54", pieced vertically)
Binding ½ yd (6 strips 2½" x 42")
Fusible Web 6 yd
Freezer Paper

Making Fused Appliqué

1. On a photocopier enlarge by 200% the pattern on page 72 for a 12" square finished block. Tape your photocopied pages together, then use freezer paper to trace a master pattern of the block. (I prefer using a pattern on one sheet of freezer paper instead of trying to trace my appliqué pieces from taped-together pages.)

2. Trace each individual pattern piece onto the paper side of your favorite fusible web. (For pieces that will be covered by another piece, add a ¼" allowance to only the portion that will be covered.) Rough-cut each of the fusible web pieces.

3. Following the manufacturer's directions, iron the fusible-web pattern pieces to the wrong sides of the appropriate fabrics.

4. Cut out all the fabric pieces on the drawn lines and carefully peel off the paper backing.

5. Fold the background square into quarters and press. Use the pressed lines as guides for centering your appliqué pieces.

6. Position each appliqué piece on the background square. Fuse the pieces to the background according to the manufacturer's instructions.

Stitching Appliqué Edges

1. Place a piece of freezer paper behind your background square to stabilize it for sewing.

2. Working in alphabetical order, machine stitch the raw edges of each piece with a narrow zigzag stitch in matching thread. Tear away the stabilizer when your appliqué is complete.

3. Press the appliquéd block.

Assembling and Finishing Your Quilt

1. These blocks can be pieced together in several different ways. I recommend you lay them out and select your favorite layout. See the assembly diagrams in figure 1 for some layout options.

2. Once you have selected your favorite layout, sew the appliqué blocks together to form rows. Use ¼" seam allowances when piecing the blocks together. Sew the rows together to form the quilt top.

3. Layer the quilt top, batting, and backing. Baste the layers together. Quilt as desired. Bind the edges to finish.

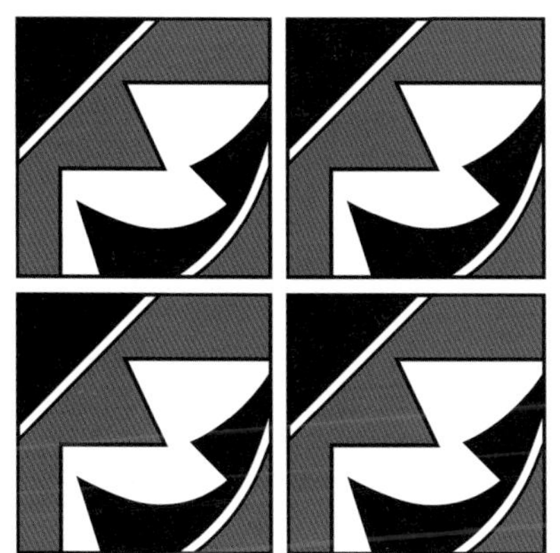

Fig. 1. Three different layout options for the Ancient Acoma block

Fig. 2. Ancient Acoma quilt assembly

Fig. 3. An alternate colorway for Ancient Acoma block

Ancient Acoma Pattern

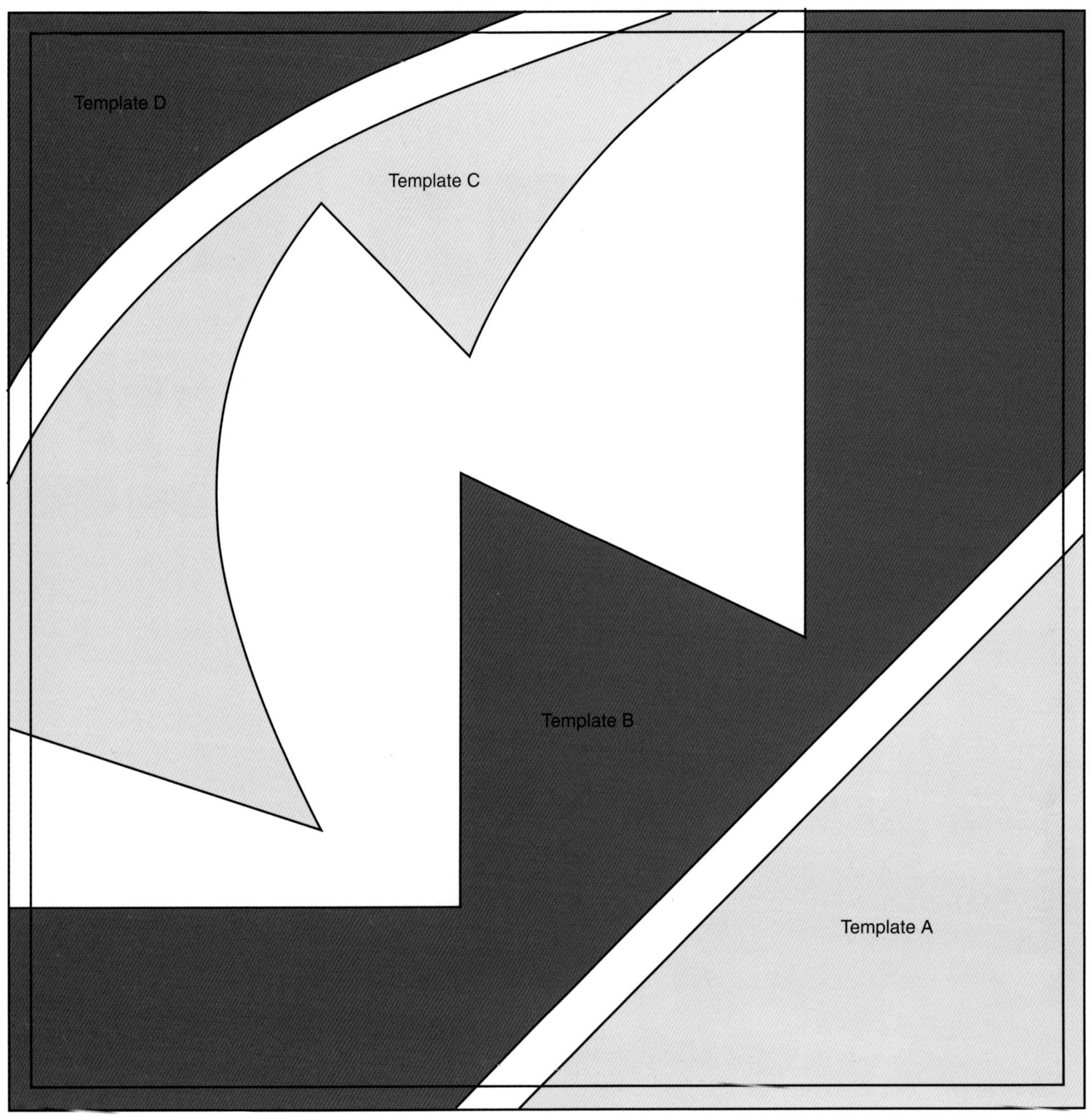

Enlarge 200%

Bears and Bear Paws

Bears and Bear Paws 80" x 94". Made by the author and Marion Wessel, Roswell, New Mexico. Quilted by Richard Larson, Plano, Texas. Block size: 14" x 14".

The Bear Paw block is a traditional block that has several variations. I selected my favorite variation and combined it with a simple bear appliqué block. My simple bear, a symbol of strength, is inspired by the bear fetishes I collect. A fetish is a small carved figure, usually an animal made of stone, and is thought to bring good luck. People from all over the world have made and used fetishes since the beginning of time. The Zuni are among the most skillful carvers, producing some of the most appealing figures today.

A heart line is a line from the mouth to the torso and it represents the path of the breath. The heart line can be hand or machine embroidered, or appliquéd.

Fabric requirements and cutting instructions

Light Print 2 yd

Pieced Blocks

Cut 4 strips 6½" x 42"
From these, cut 60 strips 2½" x 6½"
Cut 9 strips 2⅞" x 42"
From these, cut 120 squares 2⅞" x 2⅞"
Cut 4 strips 2½" x 42"
From these, cut 60 squares 2½" x 2½"

Red Print 2⅞ yd

Pieced Blocks

Cut 8 strips 4½" x 42"
From these, cut 60 squares 4½" x 4½"
Cut 9 strips 2⅞" x 42"
From these, cut 120 squares 2⅞" x 2⅞"
Cut 1 strip 2½" x 42"
From this, cut 15 squares 2½" x 2½"

Pieced Outer Border

Cut 5 strips 4⅞" x 42"
From these, cut 38 squares 4⅞" x 4⅞"
Cut 1 strip 3½" x 42"
From this, cut 4 strips 3½" x 4½"

Gold 4⅞ yd

Appliqué Background

Cut 8 strips 16" x 42"
From these, cut 15 squares 16" x 16"

Pieced Outer Border

Cut 5 strips 4⅞" x 42"
From these, cut 38 squares 4⅞" x 4⅞"
Cut 1 strip 4½" x 42"
From this, cut 4 squares 4½" x 4½"
Cut 1 strip 3½" x 42"
From this, cut 4 squares 3½" x 3½"

Black 2 yd

Appliqué Pieces

15 pieces from template A

Inner Border

8 strips 1½" x 42"

Batting 86" x 100"

Backing 7⅝ yd
(3 lengths 86", pieced horizontally)

Binding ¾ yd (9 strips 2½" x 42")

Fusible Web 4 yd

Freezer Paper

Making Fused Appliqué Bear Blocks

1. On a photocopier, enlarge by 200% the pattern on page 78 for a 14" square finished block. Tape your photocopied pages together, then use freezer paper to trace a master pattern of the block. (I prefer using a pattern on one sheet of freezer paper instead of trying to trace my appliqué pieces from taped-together pages.)

2. Trace the bear pattern onto the paper side of your favorite fusible web.

3. Following the manufacturer's directions, iron the fusible web pattern pieces to the wrong sides of the black fabric. Cut out the bears along the drawn lines and carefully peel off the paper backing.

4. Fold the background square into quarters and press. Use the pressed lines as guides for centering your appliqué piece.

5. Center the bear on the background square. Fuse it to the background according to the manufacturer's instructions.

Stitching appliqué edges

1. Place a piece of freezer paper behind your background square to stabilize it for sewing.

2. Machine stitch the raw edges of the bear piece with a narrow zigzag stitch in matching thread. Tear away the stabilizer when your appliqué is complete. Make 15 bear blocks (see the quilt assembly diagram on page 77).

3. Hand or machine embroider the arrow design on the bear. The arrow design can also be appliquéd if desired.

4. Press the appliquéd block, then trim it to 14½" x 14½", which includes seam allowances.

Making the Pieced Bear Paw Blocks

1. Sew 120 pairs of 2⅞" red and light print squares with diagonal lines of stitching. (See Tips on Piecing Half-Square Triangles on page 8.) From these, cut 240 half-square triangle units (fig. 1).

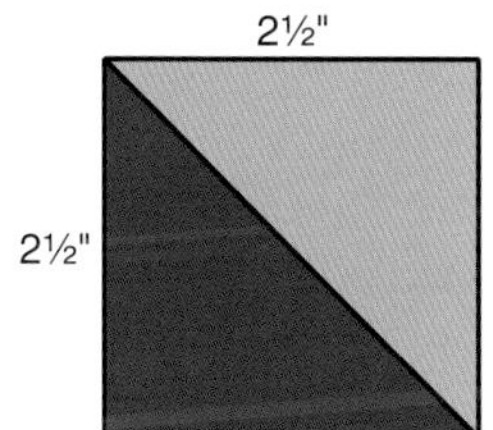

Fig. 1. Cut 240 half-square triangle units.

2. Use the units from step 1, the light print 2½" squares, and the red 4½" squares to assemble the units shown in figure 2.

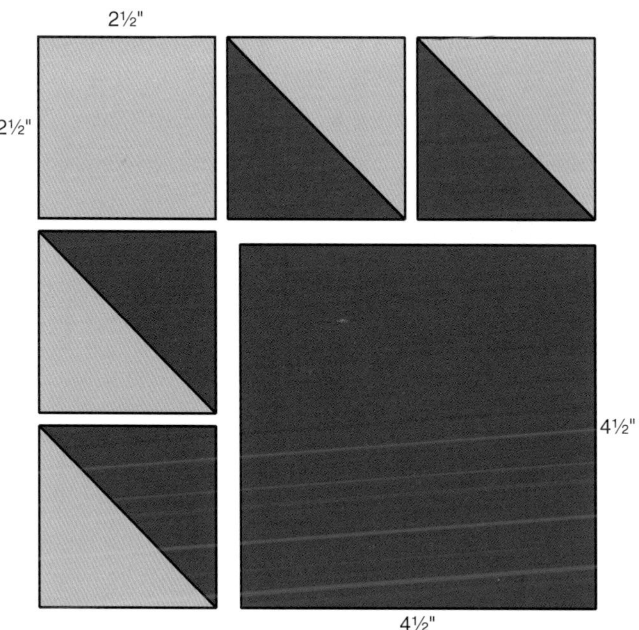

Fig. 2. Assemble 60 units.

3. Assemble 15 Bear Paw blocks (fig.3).

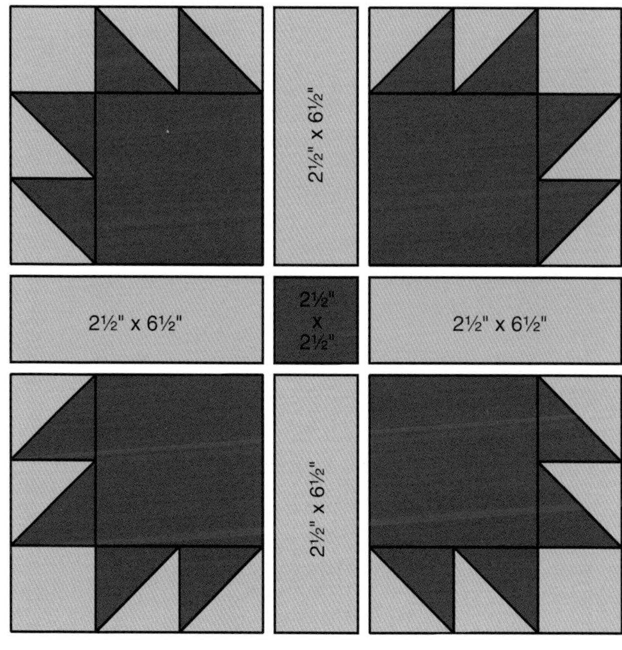

Fig. 3. Assemble 15 Bear Paw blocks.

Assembling Your Quilt Top

1. Referring to the quilt assembly diagram on page 77, join the blocks in rows. Use 1/4" seam allowances when piecing the blocks together. Press the seam allowances in rows 1, 3, and 5 to the left. Press the seam allowances in rows 2, 4, and 6 to the right. Sew the rows together to form the quilt top.

2. Using diagonal seams, sew the black inner border strips together to form one long strip. Cut 2 strips 1½" x 70½" and sew them to the top and bottom edges of the quilt, according to the assembly diagram. Cut two strips 1½" x 86½" and sew them to the right and left sides of the quilt, according to the assembly diagram. Press the seam allowances outward.

Making the Pieced Borders and Finishing Your Quilt

Pieced border for the quilt

1. Sew 38 pairs of 4⅞" red and gold squares with diagonal rows of stitching. (See Tips on Piecing Half-Square Triangles on page 8.) From these, cut 76 half-square triangle units (fig. 4).

2. For the side borders, using one 3½" gold square and a 3½" x 4½" red piece, make two left-side corner square units (fig. 5a). Piece two similar right-side corner square units (fig. 5b) Assemble these into two units as shown in figure 5c).

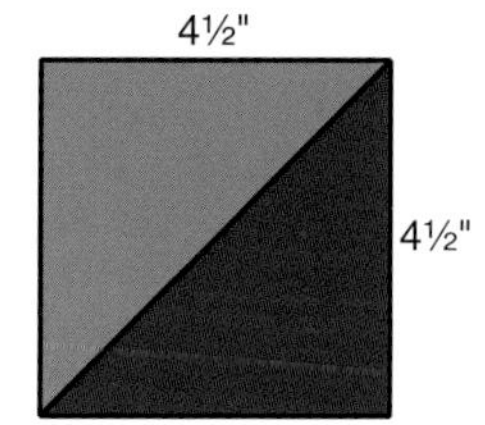

Fig. 4. Cut 76 units.

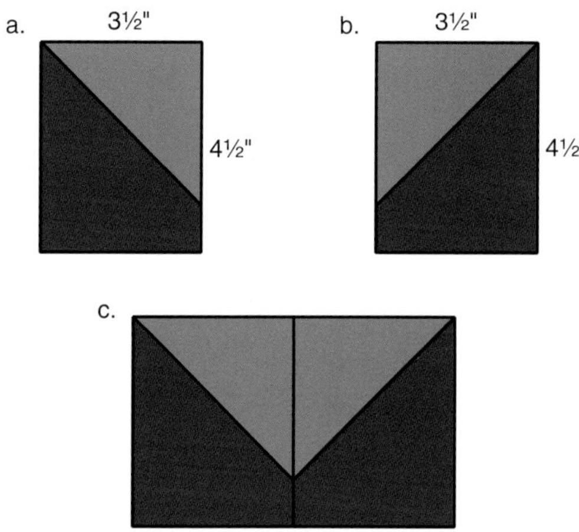

Fig. 5. (a.) Make two left-side units. (b.) Make two right-side units. (c.) Assemble two border units.

3. For the top and bottom of the quilt, assemble two pieced border units as shown in figure 6a. These border units should measure 4½" x 72½". Sew them to the top and bottom edges of the quilt top, as shown in the assembly diagram on page 77. Press the seam allowances outward.

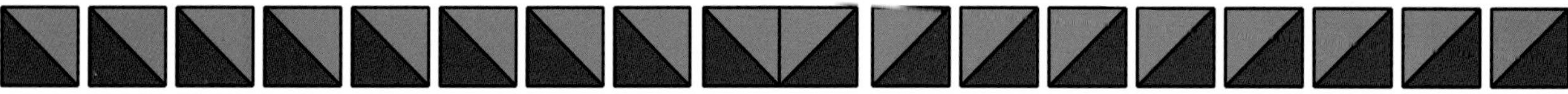

Top and bottom borders

Fig. 6a. Assemble two of each for the top and bottom of the quilt.

Left and right side borders

Fig. 6b. Add the 4½" gold squares. Assemble two of each .

4. For the right and left sides of the quilt, add the 4½" gold squares (fig. 6b). The right- and left-side border strips should measure 4½" x 94½". Sew the border strips to each side of the quilt top. Press seam allowances open.

5. Layer quilt top, batting and backing. Baste layers together. Quilt as desired. Bind edges to finish.

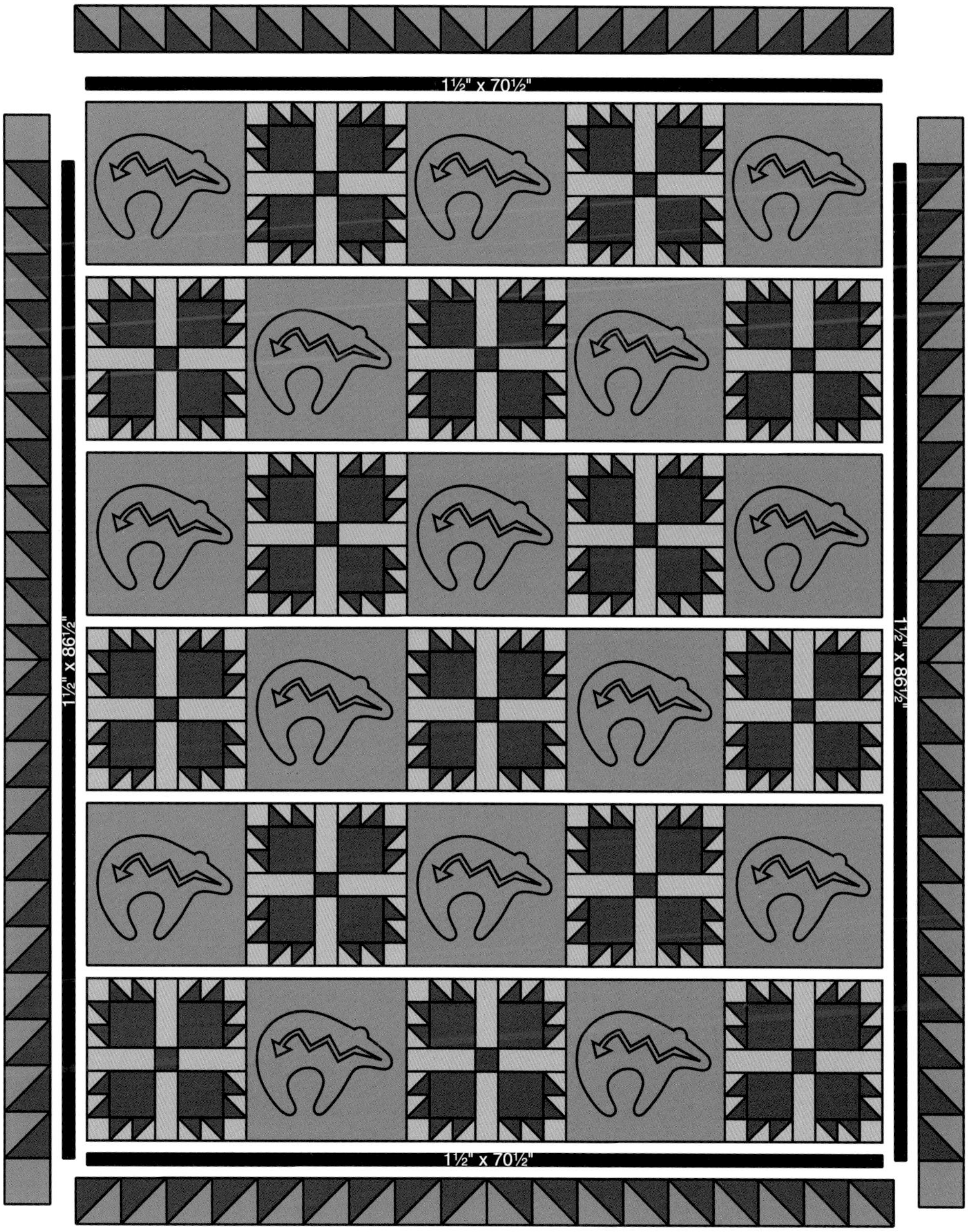

Fig. 7. Bears and Bear Paws quilt assembly

Bears and Bear Paws Pattern

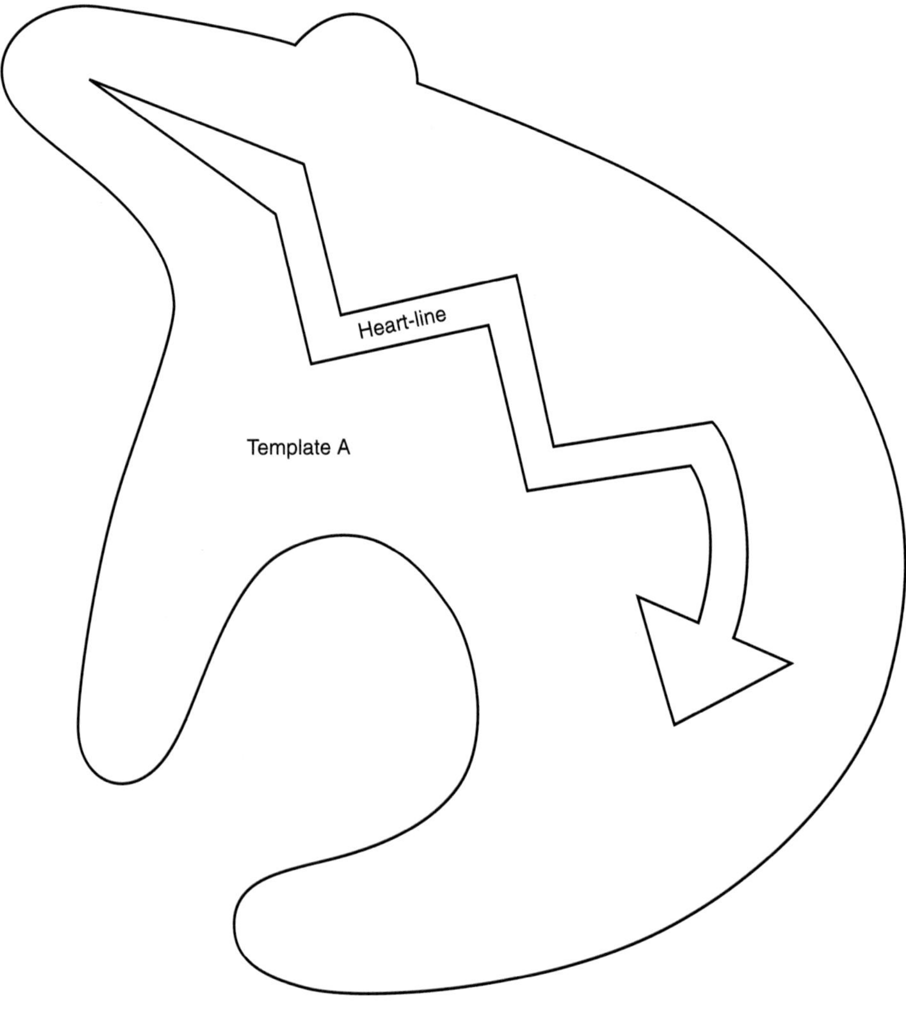

Enlarge 200%

Feathered Plates

Feathered Plates, 60" x 77". Made by the author. Quilted by Rita Galaska, Alto, New Mexico. Block size: 17" x 17".

A simple wedge shape is used to make the age old favorite Dresden Plate block. I have taken a single feather shape and appliquéd it into a graceful circle. The feather design is a very common motif used in many Native American arts. The feather shape I used is inspired by pottery designs.

Fabric requirements and cutting

Yardages are based on 42" wide fabric. All strips are cut across the width of the fabric.

Beige Swirl Batik 4¼ yd

Background
Cut 6 strips 19" x 42"
From these, cut 12 squares 19" x 19"

Outer Border
7 strips 3½" x 42"

Gray 2¾ yd

Appliqué Pieces
144 pieces from template B
12 pieces from template C

Inner Border
7 strips 2" x 42"

Gold ¾ yd

Appliqué Pieces
144 pieces from template A

Batting 75" x 82"
Backing 4⅞ yd (2 lengths 83" pieced vertically)
Binding ⅝ yd (7 strips 2½" x 42")
Fusible Web 5 yd
Freezer Paper

Making Fused Appliqué

1. Make templates of appliqué pieces A, B, and C on page 82. This is one quarter of the 17" square finished block. Trace the pattern onto a piece of freezer paper.

2. Trace each individual pattern piece onto the paper side of your favorite fusible web. (For pieces that will be covered by another piece, add a ¼" allowance to only the portion that will be covered.) Rough-cut each of the fusible web pieces.

3. Following the manufacturer's directions, iron the fusible-web pattern pieces to the wrong sides of the appropriate fabrics.

4. Cut out all the fabric pieces along the drawn lines and carefully peel off the paper backing.

5. Fold the background squares into quarters and press. Use the pressed lines as guides for centering your appliqué pieces on your fabric.

6. Referring to the appliqué layout diagram in figure 1 on page 81, position each appliqué piece on the background square. Fuse the pieces to the background according to the manufacturer's instructions.

Stitching Appliqué Edges

1. Place a piece of freezer paper behind your background square to stabilize it for sewing.

2. In alphabetical order, machine stitch the raw edges of each piece with a narrow zigzag stitch in matching thread. Tear away the stabilizer when your appliqué is complete.

3. Press the appliquéd block, then trim it to 17½" x 17½", which includes seam allowances.

Fig. 1. Appliqué layout

Finishing Your Feathered Plates Quilt

1. Sew the 17½" blocks into rows, according to the quilt assembly diagram on page 83. Use ¼" seam allowances when piecing blocks together. Press the seam allowances in rows 1 and 3 to the left. Press the seam allowances in rows 2 and 4 to the right. Sew the rows together to form the quilt top.

2. Using diagonal seams, sew the seven gray inner border strips together to form a long strip. Cut the long strip into:

2 strips 2" x 77½"
2 strips 2" x 51½"
4 strips 2" x 3½"

3. Using diagonal seams, sew the seven beige swirl batik border strips together to form a long strip. Cut the long strip into:

2 strips 3½" x 68½"
2 strips 3½" x 51½"
4 squares 3½" x 3½"

4. Referring to the assembly diagram, sew the border strips from steps 2 and 3 to the quilt top. Press the seam allowances outward.

5. Layer the quilt top, batting, and backing. Baste the layers together. Quilt as desired. Bind the edges to finish.

Feathered Plates full-sized pattern

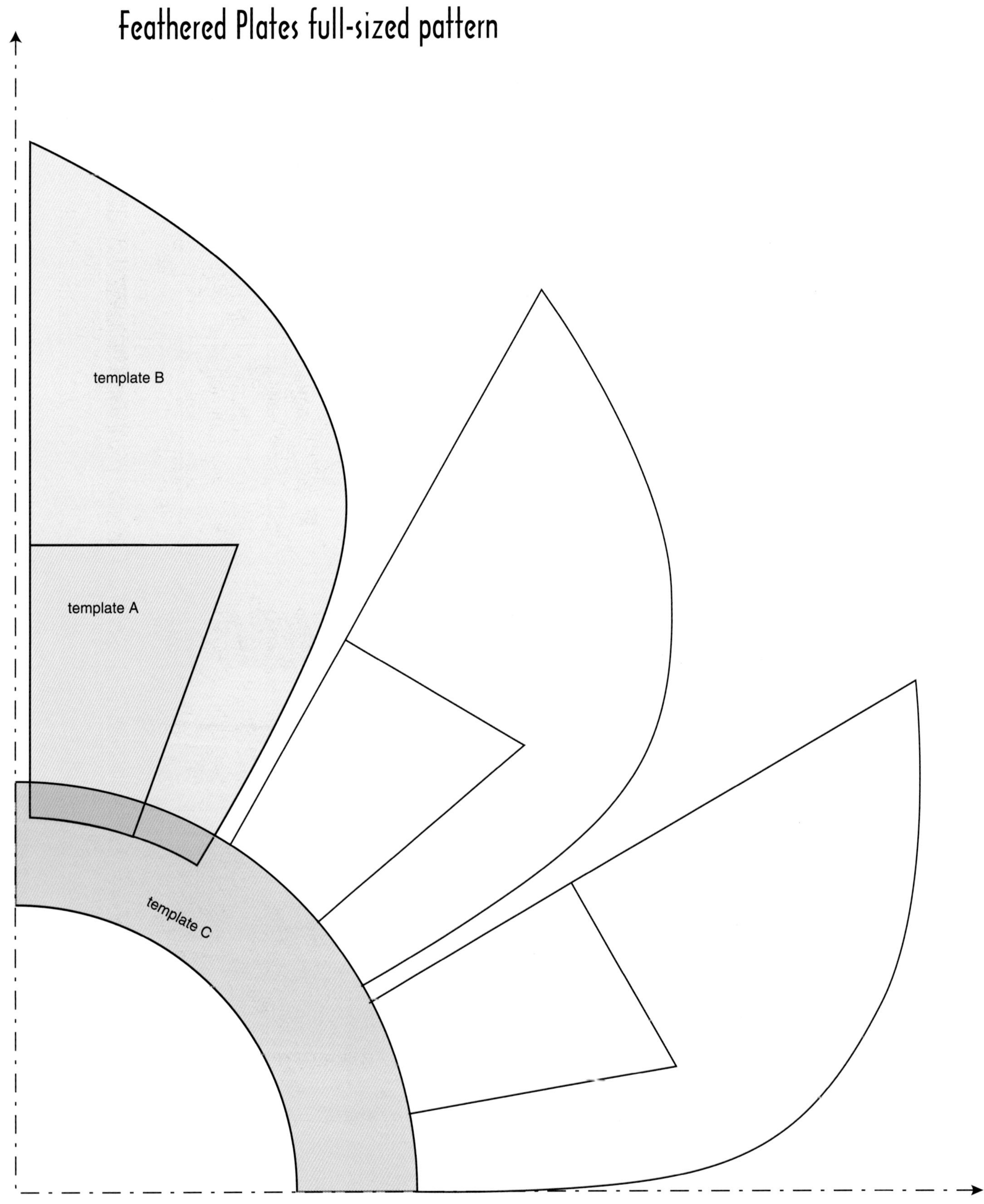

Fig. 2. Feathered Plates assembly diagram

Fig. 3. An alternate colorway for FEATHERED PLATES block

Finding Inspiration

The FEATHERED PLATE appliqué design was inspired by patterns found on pottery. The fabric selections for this quilt were inspired by the colors seen in the desert landscapes.

Mexican Talavera

MEXICAN TALAVERA 53" x 68". Appliquéd by the author. Quilted by Phillis Kent, Los Lunas, New Mexico. Block size: 15" x 15".

This appliquéd block was inspired by the Mexican Talavera tile that is so popular throughout the Southwest, where it can be seen in many homes and buildings. Talavera is a term used to describe the china and pottery made in the Spanish village of Talavera de la Reina. This style of enameled earthenware dates back to the sixteenth-century colonial era, when it was introduced to Mexico by the Spanish. The state of Puebla is the home of "authentic" Mexican Talavera pottery, where the first potters' guilds were formed to set standards and regulations for the production of Talavera and were designed to maintain uniform quality, distinctive style, and excellence. Mexican Talavera design is strongly influenced by the Orient, Italian Renaissance, the Moors, Spain, and the native people of Mexico. Talavera-style pottery is produced in many different regions of the country, resulting in a variety of different styles and designs.

Fabric requirements and cutting

Yardages are based on 42" wide fabric. All strips are cut across the width of the fabric.

Dark Blue 4 yd

Block Background
Cut 6 strips 17" x 42"
From these, cut 12 squares 17" x 17"

Appliqué Pieces
12 pieces from template D

Outer Border
Cut 7 strips 3½" x 42"

Light Blue 2 yd

Appliqué Pieces
12 pieces from template A

Inner Border
Cut 6 strips 1½" x 42"

White 3 yd

Appliqué Pieces
12 pieces from template B

Coral 1⅓ yd

Appliqué Pieces
48 pieces from template C
48 pieces from template E
48 pieces from template F

Backing 3⅝ yd
(2 lengths 61" pieced horizontally)

Batting 60" x 74"

Binding ⅝" yd (7 strips 2½" x 42")

Fusible Web 9 yd

Freezer Paper

Making Fused Appliqué

1. Trace the MEXICAN TALAVERA pattern on page 90 onto a piece of freezer paper. This one quarter of your block.

2. Trace each individual pattern piece onto the paper side of your favorite fusible web. (For pieces that will be covered by another piece, add a ¼" allowance to only the portion that will be covered.) Rough-cut each of the fusible web pieces.

3. Following the manufacturer's directions, iron the fusible-web pattern pieces to the wrong sides of the appropriate fabrics.

4. Cut out all the fabric pieces along the drawn lines and carefully peel off the paper backing.

5. Fold the background square into quarters and press. Use the pressed lines as guides for centering your appliqué pieces on your fabric.

6. Referring to the appliqué layout diagram in figure 1, position each appliqué piece on the background square. Fuse the pieces to the background according to the manufacturer's instructions.

Fig. 1. Appliqué layout

Stitching Appliqué Edges

1. Place a piece of freezer paper behind your background square to stabilize it for sewing.

2. In alphabetical order, machine stitch the raw edges of each piece with a narrow zigzag stitch in matching thread. Tear away the stabilizer when your appliqué is complete.

3. Press the appliquéd block, then trim it to 15½" x 15½", which includes seam allowances.

Finishing Your Quilt

1. Sew the 15½" blocks into rows, according to the quilt assembly diagram on page 89. Use ¼" seam allowances when piecing blocks together. Press the seam allowances in rows 1 and 3 to the left. Press the seam allowances in rows 2 and 4 to the right. Sew the rows together to form the quilt top.

2. Using diagonal seams, sew the six light blue inner border strips together to form one long strip. Cut two strips, each 1½" x 45½". Sew border strips to the top and bottom edges of the quilt top, as shown on page 89. Press the seam allowances outward. Cut two strips, each 1½" x 62½". Sew the border strips to each side of the quilt. Press the seam allowances outward.

3. Using diagonal seams, sew the seven blue outer border strips together to form one long strip. Cut two strips, each 3½" x 47½". Sew these border strips to the top and bottom of the quilt top. Press the seam allowances outward. Cut two strips, each 3½" x 68½". Sew these border strips to each side of the quilt top. Press the seam allowances outward.

4. Layer the quilt top, batting, and backing. Baste the layers together. Quilt as desired. Bind the edges to finish.

STRAWBERRY KITCHEN table runner. Made by Glenda Raby, Roswell, New Mexico.

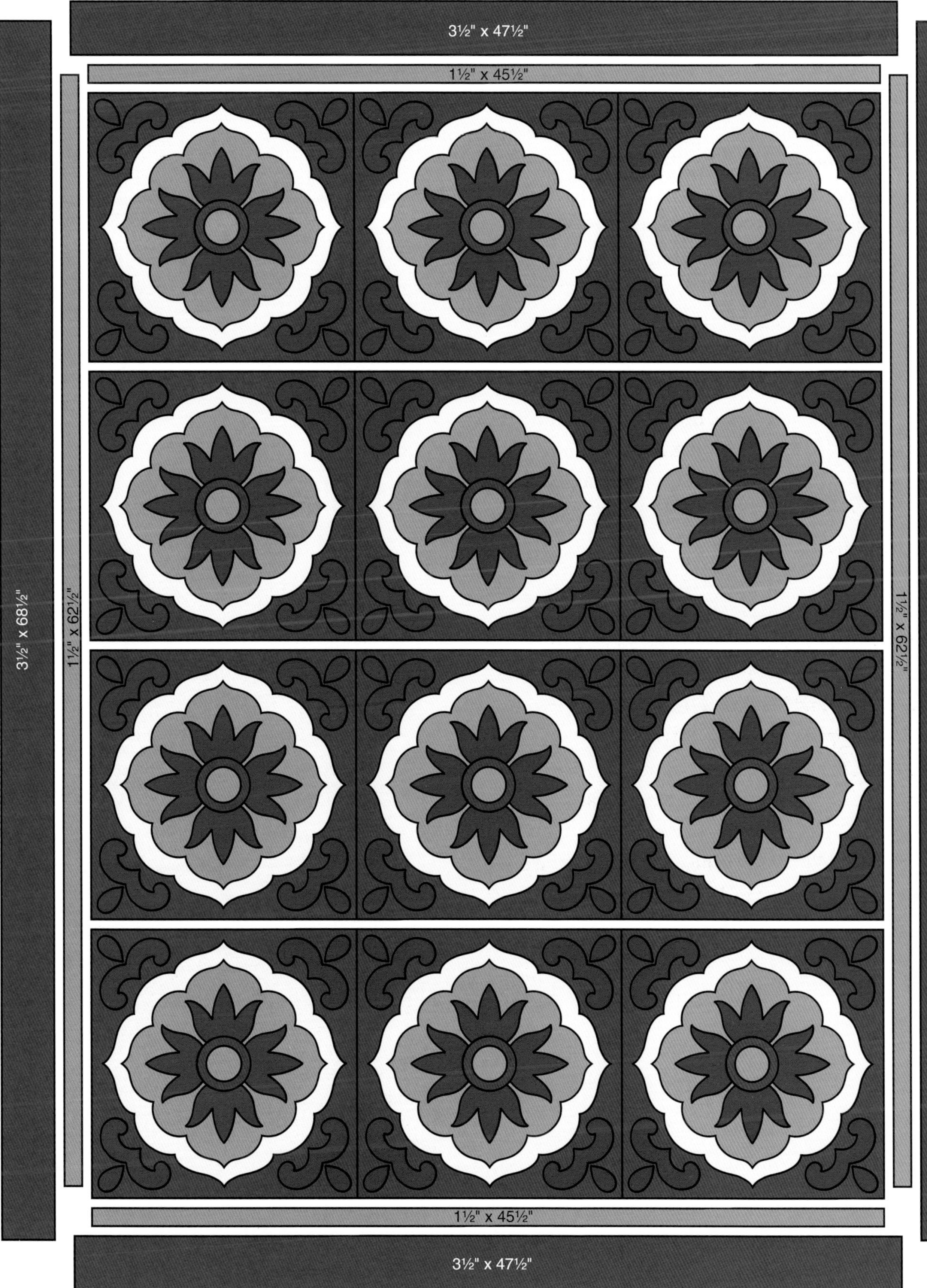

Fig. 2. Mexican Talavera quilt assembly

Mexican Talavera full-sized pattern

Fig. 3. An alternate colorway for Mexican Talavera block

Finding Inspiration

Casa Talavera, my favorite tile shop, is a feast for the eyes. It's full of colorful hand painted tiles, wall decorations, and home accessories. The shelves are full of hundreds of multicolored and two-color patterns to choose from. Many of these wonderful tile designs can easily be interpreted into unique appliquéd quilt blocks. A few simple tiles beautifully accent this hand-carved door. The repetition of a single tile design can lead to exciting discoveries, as new designs appear. A wicker chair, a lovely quilt, and coordinating art complete this peaceful room setting.

Resources

Fabrics

Southwest Decoratives
Visit the retail store or the Web site for southwest fabrics and patterns, the ultimate source for all your southwest projects.
5711 Carmel Ave. NE, Suite B
Albuquerque, New Mexico 87113
1-800-530-8995
www.swdecoratives.com

Longarm Quilters

Quilting Design Studio
Richard Larson
221 West Parker Road, Suite 410
Plano, Texas 75023
(972) 422-0768
www.qdstudio.com

Cotton Comforts
Rita Galaska
PO Box 814
Alto, New Mexico 88312
(505) 336-4375

Edith Stanton
Artesia Quilt Quarters
2101 Deeanna Lane
Midland, Texas 79707
(432) 697-2219
eastanton1@sbcglobal.net

Kokopelli Quilting Company
5711 Carmel Ave. NE, Suite B
Albuquerque, New Mexico 87113
(505) 821-7400
swd@swdecoratives.com

Places of Interest

Gathering of Nations
This is an annual celebration featuring Native American dance, music, arts and crafts.
www.gatheringofnations.com

Indian Pueblo Cultural Center
This is the gateway to information about the life, culture, history, and traditions of 19 Pueblos of New Mexico. The center features a 10,000 square foot museum of authentic history and artifacts of traditional Pueblo culture and their contemporary art.
2401 12th Street NW (1 block north of I-40)
Albuquerque, New Mexico 87104
(505) 843-7270
1-800-766-4405 (outside New Mexico)
www.indianpueblo.com

Indian Arts and Crafts Association
This is an international organization with a mission of "promoting, preserving, and protecting" Native American creations.
www.iaca.com

Bibliography

Bahti, Mark Tomas. *Southwest Indian Designs: With Some Explanations.* Baldwin Park, CA: Gem Guides Book Company, 2001.

Bonar, Eulalie H. (editor), and National Museum of the American Indian. *Woven by the Grandmothers: Nineteenth-Century Navajo Textiles from the National Museum of the American Indian.* Washington, D.C.: Smithsonian Books, 1996.

Davis, Carolyn O'Bagy. *Treasured Earth: Hattie Cosgrove's Mimbres Archaeology in the American Southwest.* Tucson, AZ: Sanpete Publications, 1995.

Eaton, Linda B. *Native American Art of the Southwest.* Lincolnwood, IL: Publications International, 1993.

Fisher, Nora. *Rio Grande Textiles.* Santa Fe, NM: Museum of New Mexico Press, 1994.

Kaufman, Alice and Christopher Selser. *The Navajo. Weaving Tradition.* Tulsa, OK: Council Oak Books, 1999.

Mori, Joyce. *Native American Designs 2.* Paducah, KY: American Quilter's Society, 2005.

National Museum of the American Indian. *This Path We Travel: Celebrations of Contemporary Native American Creativity.* Golden, CO: Fulcrum Publishing, 1994.

Patterson, Alex. *Hopi Pottery Symbols.* Boulder, CO: Johnson Books, 1994.

Rodee, Marian E. *Weaving of the Southwest.* Altgen, PA: Schiffer Publishing, 1987.

Wheat, Joe Ben. *Blanket Weaving in the Southwest.* Tucson, AZ: University of Arizona Press, 2003.

About the Author

Michelle joined the Pecos Valley Quilters in 1983 and has been busy quilting ever since. She began her quilting career when she got married and needed something to do in her free time. She started out, like most beginners, with traditional block patterns, hand piecing, and hand quilting. She soon decided to perfect her machine piecing and machine quilting skills so she could make more quilts. Michelle's talent for designing quilts and wearable art has led her to many successful endeavors. She designs and markets a line of southwestern quilt patterns. She loves sharing the beauty of the Southwest through the quilts and wearable art she designs. She has exhibited her wearable art creations in several American Quilter's Society Fashion Shows, the 1999 Fairfield Fashion Show, ARTWEAR 2002, the 2005 Bernina Fashion Show, and other regional shows. Her quilts and wearable art have been shown in galleries, museums, and quilt shows throughout the United States. Michelle teaches, lectures, and provides special exhibits for quilt groups across the country.

Michelle lives in Roswell, New Mexico, with her husband, Randy, daughter, Jessica, two pet prairie dogs, and two dogs. When she's not quilting, she enjoys spending time with her friends and family and playing with her prairie dogs, Bubba and Max.

If you would like more information about Michelle's southwestern quilt designs, you can visit her Web site at www.jmichellewatts.com or contact her at jmichelle@cableone.net.

Other AQS Books

This is only a small selection of the books available from the American Quilter's Society. AQS books are known worldwide for timely topics, clear writing, beautiful color photos, and accurate illustrations and patterns. The following books are available from your local bookseller, quilt shop, or public library.

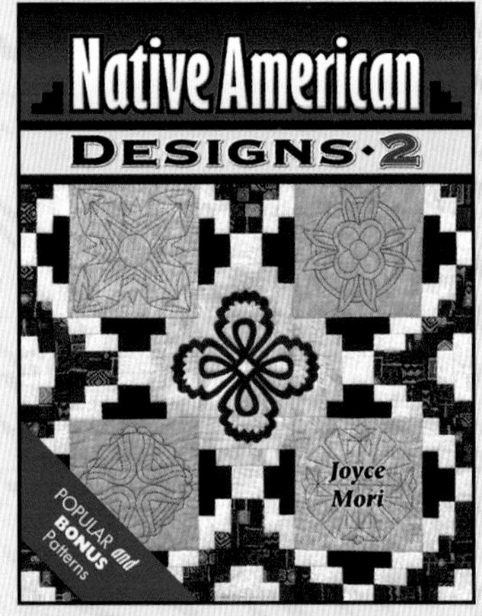

#6808 us$22.95

#6519 4¼" x 11" us$21.95

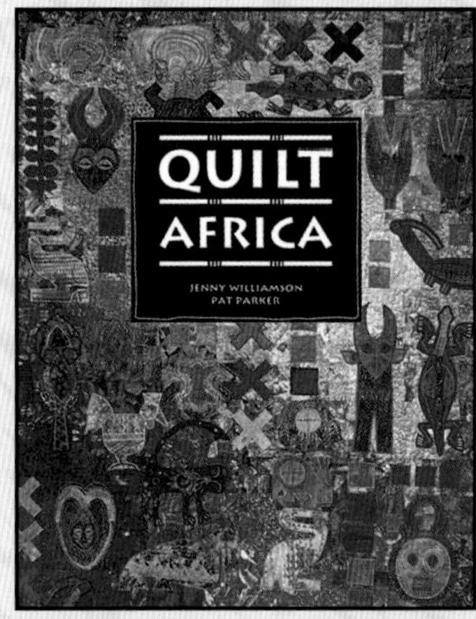

#6510 us$21.95

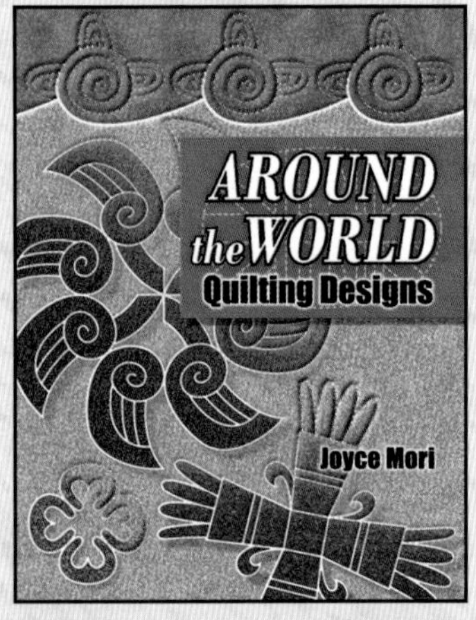

#6806 us$21.95

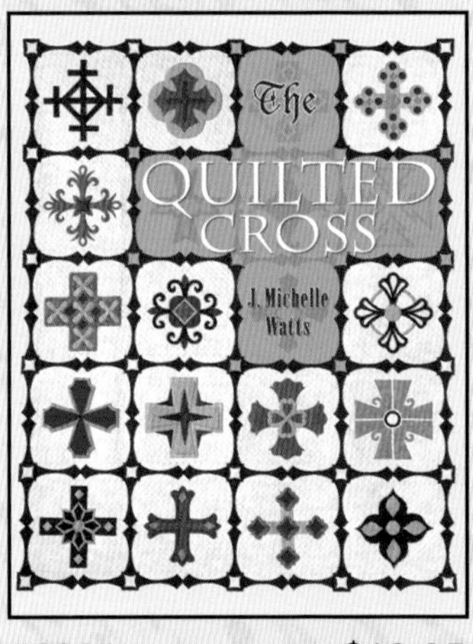

#6301 us$18.95

#6680 us$21.95

#6805 us$22.95

#6413 4¼" x 11" us$21.95

#6009 us$19.95

LOOK for these books nationally. **CALL 1-800-626-5420**
or **VISIT** our Web site at **www.AmericanQuilter.com**